DATE DUE

W-2			
APR 0 6 1987			
2 8 1988			
NOV 2 9 1988			
DEC 6 1988			

DEMCO 38-297

JAPAN

Forrest R. Pitts

Dr. Forrest R. Pitts is a well-known geographer and the author of geographical books and articles. He is Professor of Geography at the University of Hawaii. Dr. Pitts has studied and traveled in Japan in recent years. His background of study and travel helps him to describe the land and the people of Japan in an authentic and interesting manner.

Earlier Edition Copyright The Fideler Company 1979

LIBRARY OF CONGRESS CATALOG CARD NUMBER: 80-69169
ISBN: 0-88296-120-9

FIDELER SOCIAL STUDIES

World Cultures (Basic Area Studies)

(Individual books)

BRITISH ISLES	GERMANY
FRANCE	SOVIET UNION
INDIA	SOUTHEAST ASIA
CHINA	JAPAN
AFRICA	SOUTH AMERICA

The United States

American Neighbors

Inquiring About Freedom

THE FIDELER COMPANY Grand Rapids, Michigan / Toronto, Canada

JAPAN

CONTRIBUTORS

ROBERT B. HALL, Jr.
Professor of History
and Geography
University of Rochester

Betty-Jo Buell

Margaret DeWitt

Raymond E. Fideler

Margaret F. Hertel

Jerry E. Jennings

Beverly M. Miller

Mary Mitus

Carol S. Prescott

Bev J. Roche

Marion H. Smith

Joanna Van Zoest

Audrey Witham

The Ginza at night. The Ginza is the main shopping district of Tokyo, Japan's capital and largest city. Japan is one of the most densely populated countries in the world.

CONTENTS

A view from Miyajima, a sacred island in the Inland Sea near Hiroshima. The archway standing in the water indicates that there is a Shinto temple on the island.

A Global View of Asia

If you could view the earth from a space station, you would notice that its curved surface is covered mainly with water. Lying like enormous islands in the water are several great masses of land. By far the largest of these masses is Eurasia, which is located on the opposite side of the earth from North America.

Human beings have been living in Eurasia for at least one million years. Long ago, the people in the western-most part of this landmass developed a civilization that differed greatly from the civilizations in the eastern part. As time went on, the western part of Eurasia came to be called Europe. The rest of this landmass came to be known as Asia, or the East. Geographers today generally agree that Europe and Asia are divided by an imaginary line extending from the Caspian Sea northward along the Ural Mountains to the Arctic Ocean. To the south, Europe and Asia are separated by the Caucasus Mountains and by the Black and Aegean seas. (See map at right.)

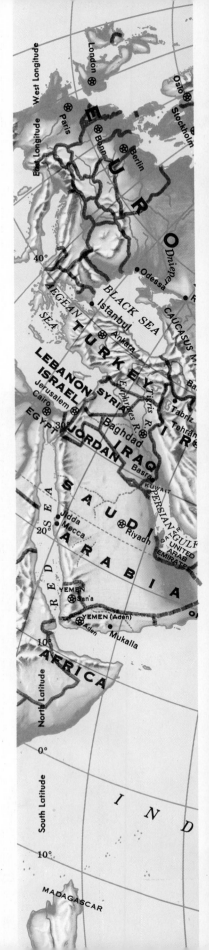

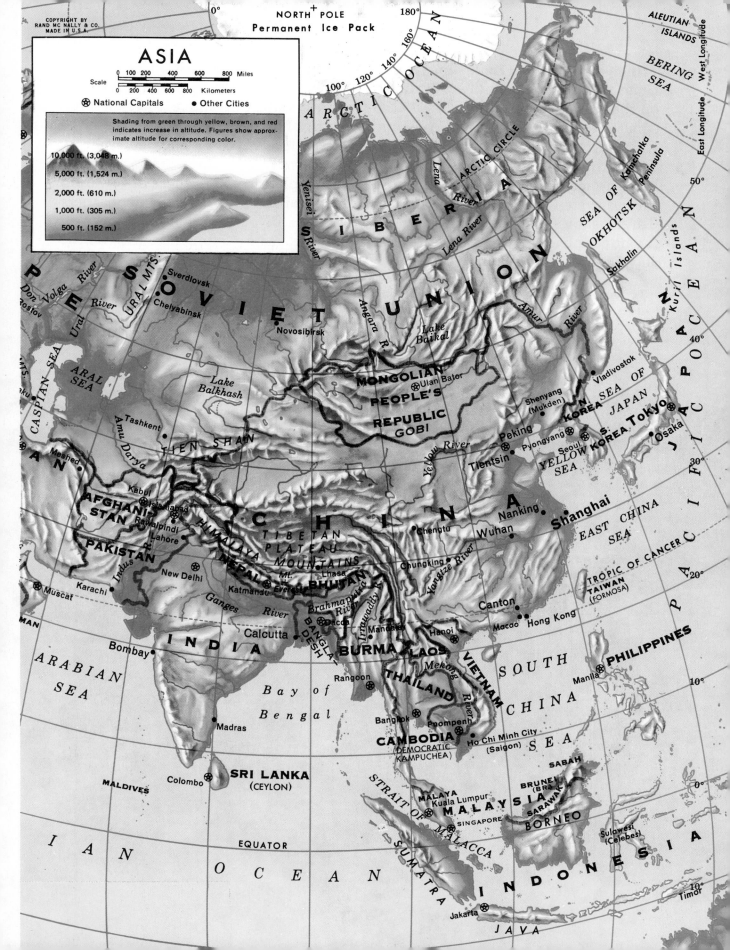

The world's largest continent. Asia is larger than any of the other continents on the earth. It extends from below the equator to above the Arctic Circle, and stretches nearly halfway around the world. About one third of the total land surface of the globe is included in this giant continent. The map on pages 6 and 7 shows that there are many different countries in Asia. Some are large and some are very small.

A continent of contrasts. The map on pages 6 and 7 also shows that Asia has a great variety of land features. In some parts of this vast continent, there are broad, level lowlands and deep valleys. In other places, there are high, windswept plateaus and ranges of towering mountains. These highland barriers help to divide the continent of Asia into six main regions. The map on the opposite page shows these regions.

Terraced mountain slopes in the Philippines, an island country off the coast of Asia. Besides the Philippines, many other islands and groups of islands are located near this giant continent. Find some of these islands on the map on pages 6 and 7.

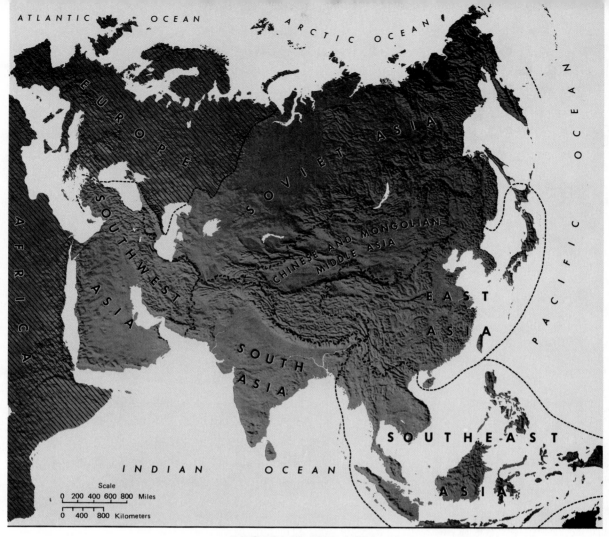

REGIONS OF ASIA

East Asia includes Japan, North and South Korea, and much of China. Taiwan and Hong Kong are located here also. There are more people living in East Asia than in any other part of the world.

Southeast Asia is a tropical, rainy region made up of islands and peninsulas. It includes the countries of Burma, Thailand, Cambodia (officially Democratic Kampuchea), Laos, Vietnam, Malaysia, Singapore, Indonesia, and the Philippines, as well as the British-protected territory of Brunei.

South Asia includes the large, triangle-shaped peninsula on which the countries of India, Pakistan, and Bangladesh are located. It also includes the island countries of the Maldives and Sri Lanka (formerly Ceylon) and the three mountainous countries of Afghanistan, Nepal, and Bhutan. South Asia is one of the most densely populated parts of the world.

Chinese and Mongolian Middle Asia includes the Mongolian People's Republic as well as Sinkiang, Inner Mongolia, and Tibet, which are part of China. It is a thinly populated region of deserts, grasslands, plateaus, and high mountains.

Soviet Asia includes the vast area known as Siberia, as well as the other parts of the Soviet Union that are located on the continent of Asia. Much of this region of Asia is thinly populated.

Southwest Asia includes Turkey, Iran, Iraq, Syria, Lebanon, Israel, Jordan, part of Egypt, the countries on the Arabian Peninsula, and the island of Cyprus. Archaeologists believe civilization may have begun in this dry, rugged region. Three of the world's great religions — Judaism, Christianity, and Islam — began here. Some of the world's largest reserves of oil are located in this region.

Workers drilling for oil in Southeast Asia. Asia has a wealth of natural resources, such as rich mineral deposits, fertile farmlands, and vast forests. In most Asian countries, however, the people have not used their resources as fully as they might. You may wish to do research to discover why this is so.

A continent of rich resources. Some parts of Asia contain great natural wealth. Vast deposits of coal and petroleum are located on this continent. Asia is also rich in tin and other minerals needed by modern industry. It has large forests, and rushing rivers that could be used to produce hydroelectric power. In much of Asia, the land and climate are poor for growing crops. However, this continent also has large areas of fertile farmland.

A continent with a huge population. In a continent so large and so rich in natural resources you would expect to find many people. The map on pages 12 and 13 shows that this idea is correct. About two and one half billion people live in Asia today. This is about six tenths of the world's population.

All parts of Asia are not equally crowded. As the map on pages 12 and 13 shows, a large part of the continent has almost no people. Other parts are densely populated. Why do you think Asia's population is distributed so unevenly? The map on pages 6 and 7 and the map below provide clues that may help you answer this question.

The home of many different peoples. Asia's people are divided into hundreds of separate groups. These groups differ greatly from one another in their customs and ways of living. They also speak different languages. For example, there are fourteen major languages in India alone.

A continent with a long history. People have been living in Asia for hundreds of thousands of years. Some of the world's first civilizations arose on this continent. Asia

The amount of rainfall differs from place to place on the continent of Asia. How do you think rainfall helps to determine where people live?

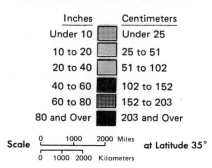

WORLD AVERAGE ANNUAL PRECIPITATION

Inches		Centimeters
Under 10		Under 25
10 to 20		25 to 51
20 to 40		51 to 102
40 to 60		102 to 152
60 to 80		152 to 203
80 and Over		203 and Over

Scale 0   1000   2000 Miles   at Latitude 35°
       0 1000 2000 Kilometers

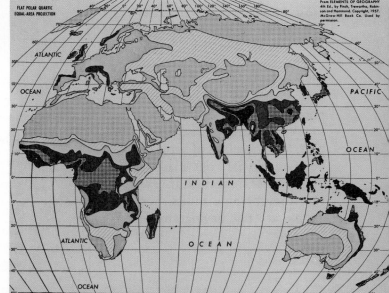

From ELEMENTS OF GEOGRAPHY 4th Ed., by Finch, Trewartha, Robinson and Hammond. Copyright, 1957. McGraw-Hill Book Co. Used by permission.

FLAT POLAR QUARTIC EQUAL-AREA PROJECTION

A crowded street in Delhi. About six tenths of the world's people live in Asia. Most of them are in South and East Asia. Why are these two areas so heavily populated?

WORLD POPULATION

About four and one-half billion people live in the world today. If all these people were distributed evenly over the earth there would be about seventy-nine people living on each square* mile of land. This is not the case, however. The map at right shows that some areas are very crowded, while others are almost empty. The three most heavily populated parts of the world are East Asia, South Asia, and Europe.

The world's population is more than twice as large as it was only fifty years ago. Larger food supplies and better medical care help to explain this increase. In the past, large numbers of babies were born each year, but many children died of hunger or disease before they became adults. Today, people are not having any more

*See Glossary

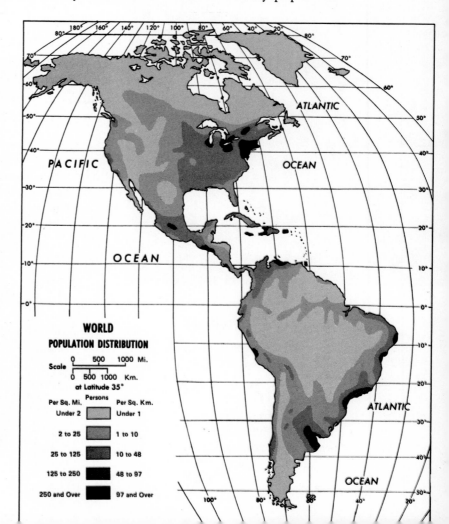

WORLD POPULATION DISTRIBUTION

Scale

0   500   1000 Mi.

0 500 1000 Km.
at Latitude 35°

Per Sq. Mi. Persons		Per Sq. Km.
Under 2		Under 1
2 to 25		1 to 10
25 to 125		10 to 48
125 to 250		48 to 97
250 and Over		97 and Over

12

children than before, but more children are living to become adults and to have families of their own. It is mainly for this reason that the world's population has been growing so rapidly. If it continues at its present rate, world population will probably double again in about thirty-five years.

The population of the developing countries is increasing more rapidly than the population of the industrialized nations, where families are generally smaller. For example, population is growing about twice as fast in the developing country of India as it is in the industrialized nation of Japan.

The rapid growth of population is a serious problem for all the people of the world. Each year, human beings are using larger and larger amounts of the earth's resources. Many experts believe that population growth must slow down if people everywhere are to have an opportunity to meet their needs.

Population distribution. The world's population is increasing at an average rate of about 1.9 percent each year. What facts help explain this? Which areas have the most rapid population growth?

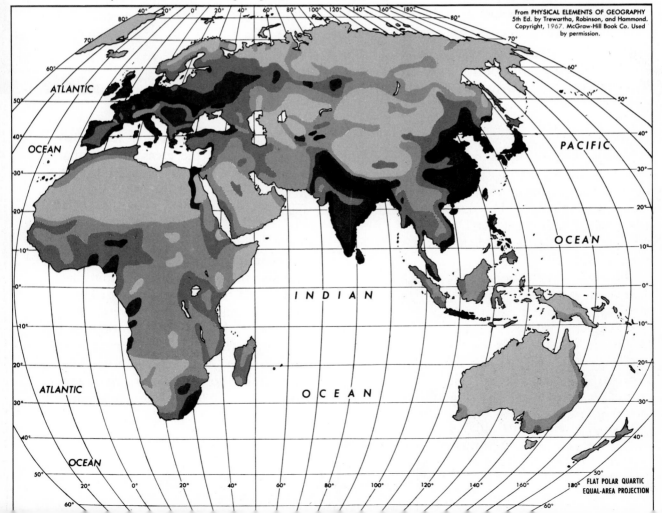

From PHYSICAL ELEMENTS OF GEOGRAPHY 5th Ed. by Trewartha, Robinson, and Hammond. Copyright, 1967. McGraw-Hill Book Co. Used by permission.

FLAT POLAR QUARTIC
EQUAL-AREA PROJECTION

has been the home of many great artists, writers, and thinkers. All of the world's major religions developed here. People in Asia produced many inventions that still affect our lives. For example, printing was invented in China, and iron making developed in what is now Turkey. Over the centuries, many great cities grew up in Asia. These cities were famous for their wealth and beauty.

A continent that has seen great changes. During the 1800's, several powerful Western* nations took over large areas in Asia. Among these countries were Great Britain, France, and the Netherlands. They had strong national governments and a great deal of industry. In most Asian countries, the national government was very weak. Many people felt more loyalty to their own small groups than they did to the nation as a whole. Also, the Asian countries had little industry. It was these weaknesses that made it possible for Western countries to take over large areas in Asia. (See map below.)

In the early years of this century, a new feeling arose in the hearts of many Asians. They wanted to form strong, independent nations of their own. This feeling is known as nationalism. As time

*See Glossary

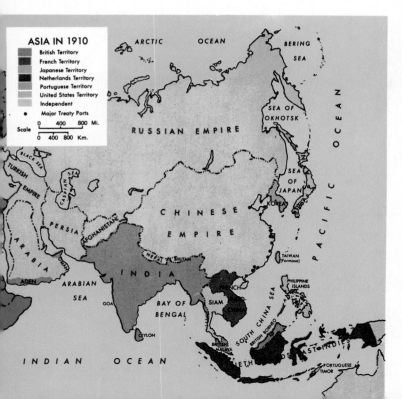

ASIA IN 1910

British Territory
French Territory
Japanese Territory
Netherlands Territory
Portuguese Territory
United States Territory
Independent
• Major Treaty Ports

Scale
0   400   800 Mi.
0   400   800 Km.

ARCTIC OCEAN
BERING SEA
SEA OF OKHOTSK
RUSSIAN EMPIRE
SEA OF JAPAN
PACIFIC OCEAN
KOREA
CHINESE EMPIRE
TAIWAN (Formosa)
BLACK SEA
TURKISH EMPIRE
CASPIAN SEA
PERSIA
AFGHANISTAN
ARABIA
NEPAL
BHUTAN
PHILIPPINE ISLANDS
ADEN
ARABIAN SEA
GOA
INDIA
BAY OF BENGAL
SIAM
FRENCH
CEYLON
SOUTH CHINA SEA
BRITISH MALAYA
BRITISH BORNEO
EAST INDIES
PORTUGUESE TIMOR
INDIAN OCEAN

Colonialism

The map at left shows the areas of Asia that were independent in 1910 and the areas that were under colonial rule. Several countries shown as independent were actually under the influence of stronger nations. For example, the great Chinese Empire had been forced to sign treaties that allowed foreign nations to control several of its seaports. During and after World War I and World War II, many changes took place in Asia. You may wish to make maps similar to this one in which you show Asia in 1930, in 1950, and today.

Refer to pages 177-179 for help in finding the information you need.

An Independence Day parade in Malaysia. During this century, Malaysia, Indonesia, and many other countries in Asia have become independent. What is the main reason for this?

passed, nationalism helped Asians to win their freedom from Western rule. Today, Asia is the home of about forty independent nations.

To see how nationalism arose in Asia, let us look at the history of Indonesia. This country is located on a group of islands in Southeast Asia. (See map on pages 6 and 7.) In early times, Indonesia was divided into many small, quarreling states. During the eighteenth century, people from the Netherlands began taking over Indonesia. They set up a strong colonial government. Later, roads, railroads, and a shipping line were established. These brought the people into closer contact with each other. Some Indonesians had a chance to attend Western schools. There they learned new ideas about freedom and self-government. They also came to realize that the Western nations were getting most of the benefit from Southeast Asia's rich resources.

All of these things helped the growth of nationalism in Indonesia. After World War II* ended, the Indonesians refused to live under foreign rule any longer. They fought hard for their independence and won it.

A continent whose people are seeking a better way of life. Independence did not solve all the problems facing the people of Asia. Today, most Asian countries are very poor. Although they have rich resources, these resources have not been fully developed. There is little modern industry. Most of the people still make their living by farming. Millions of Asians suffer from hunger and disease. There are not enough roads, schools, or hospitals.

In the past, many Asians took their poverty for granted. They did not know that there was any other way of life. This is no longer true. In movies and foreign magazines, Asians see healthy people who have better food, clothing, and housing than they do. They also see cars, television sets, and other products commonly used in Western countries. As a result, people in Asia are now demanding a better way of life for themselves.

Japan is one of the most prosperous nations in Asia. A few Asian countries have a higher standard* of living than the others. Among these is the island nation of Japan. In Japan today, most people enjoy a comfortable way of life. For example, they have enough food to eat and attractive clothes to wear. Also, most Japanese are healthy and well-educated. As you read about Japan in this book, try to discover why it has become such a prosperous nation.

A village on the island of Borneo. Most of Asia's people live in small villages and earn their living by farming. They are generally very poor. In the past, Asians took their poverty for granted, but now they are demanding a better way of life. How did this change come about?

JAPAN

An Overview of Japan

Where is Japan? Along the coasts of Asia are many islands. The island chain that lies off the middle part of Asia's eastern coast forms the country of Japan. An arm of the Pacific Ocean called the Sea of Japan separates this island country from the mainland of Asia. (See map on pages 6 and 7.)

A prosperous industrial country. Travelers who cross Asia on their way to Japan find that most of the countries through which they pass are very poor. There is little modern industry in these countries. Most of the people make their living as farmers.

When these travelers reach Japan, they feel as though they have come to a different world. Here, the people are generally prosperous. Only about one eighth of Japan's workers are employed in farming, and the number is steadily growing smaller. In the towns and cities are modern factories and offices. The city streets are bright with neon signs. Television antennas rise from the roofs of most houses.

Japan is one of the world's leading industrial powers. It ranks first among the shipbuilding countries of the world. Japan produces more steel than any other country except the United States and the Soviet Union. It is also a leading producer of motor vehicles, computers, chemicals, and textiles.

A nation that has faced great problems. The Japanese have had to overcome great problems to become as prosperous as they are today. Japan lacks many of the natural resources needed by modern industry. For instance, it is poor in iron ore, coking* coal, and other minerals. It also has little farmland. The amount of farmland seems especially small when you consider that Japan has about 117 million people to feed. As Chapter 12 explains, Japan has met the problem of limited natural resources by becoming a "workshop" nation. It imports food and raw materials from countries all over the world. In Japanese

*See Glossary

A Japanese worker welds steel plates for a giant tanker. Japan is one of the world's leading industrial powers. It ranks first among the shipbuilding countries of the world. Japan produces more steel than any other country except the United States and the Soviet Union. It is also a leading producer of motor vehicles, computers, cameras, and television sets.

factories, these raw materials are made into hundreds of useful products. Japan sells manufactured goods to other countries to pay for the food and raw materials that it imports.

Through the years, the Japanese have overcome other serious problems as well. During the 1930's, Japan's government came under the control of ambitious military leaders. These men wanted to conquer other nations and build a great empire. In 1941, Japan launched a surprise attack on a United States military base in Hawaii. This action brought Japan and the United States into World War II.*

Shopping in a Japanese supermarket. The standard* of living in Japan is much higher than it is in most other Asian countries. Japan is a small, crowded country with few natural resources. Yet it has become a prosperous industrial nation. What facts help to explain Japan's success?

The war ended with Japan's defeat in 1945. Japan was occupied by troops from the United States and other Allied* nations. When the occupation troops landed in Japan, they found an exhausted, broken country. Cities were in ruins. Factories had been destroyed, or were standing idle. Many people did not have enough food to eat. It seemed unlikely that Japan would soon recover from this destruction. But the Japanese surprised everyone. With the help of the Allied nations, they set to work rebuilding their war-torn country. In a short period of time, Japan had become more prosperous than ever before.

Japan in today's world. Today Japan plays an important part in world affairs. As you have discovered, it is a leader in industry and trade. The hardworking, inventive people of Japan have much to share with people in other nations. Japan's artists are creating valuable works of literature, music, art, and architecture. Its scientists and engineers are also making many important contributions.

Japan now serves as a helpful model for other nations in Asia. It has shown that a country with few natural resources and many people can become a prosperous industrial nation. Japan also has shown that a country with little experience in democracy can set up a successful democratic government. Today the Japanese are sharing their skills, ideas, and money with people in the developing nations. (See map on page 120.) In this way, Japan has become an active partner in the task of building a better world.

Of course, the Japanese face some of the same problems that people in other industrial countries do. Among these problems are high prices, crowded living conditions, pollution, and fuel shortages. However, the Japanese people have shown in the past that they can overcome serious problems. It seems likely that they will continue to do so in the future.

Part 1
Land and Climate

Although Japan is not a large country, it is a land of great contrasts. If you were to travel through Japan, you would see lofty, snowcapped mountains and broad, flat plains. You would see tidy farms and sprawling cities. In wintertime, you would find the land in the north blanketed with deep snow, while in the south you would find clear, sunny skies and milder temperatures. What would you like to know about Japan's land and climate? Make a list of questions you want to answer. Perhaps you would like to include the following questions on your list.

- Where is Japan located? What countries are her nearest neighbors?
- What important bodies of water border Japan?
- What are Japan's main land features?
- In what ways does Japan's climate differ from place to place and from season to season?

The chapters in Part 1 will help you discover answers to your questions. In doing research, remember that maps and pictures provide valuable information about land and climate.

Japan has some of the world's most beautiful scenery. Although it is not a large country, Japan is a land of great contrasts. Land features and climate differ greatly from place to place.

1 Land

An island country. Japan is a country of many islands. If you look at the map on the opposite page, you will see that four of these islands are quite large, while others are very small. All these islands together cover an area about as large as the state of California.

This small, island country lies off the east coast of the mainland of Asia. (See map on pages 6 and 7.) To the west is the Sea of Japan. To the east lies the Pacific Ocean. No part of Japan is more than one hundred miles from the sea.

How Japan was formed. Hills and mountains cover most of the land in Japan. This rugged, island country is the upper part of a great mountain range that rose from the bottom of the ocean. Millions of years ago, movements deep within the earth cracked the layers of rock at the bottom of the ocean and pushed them upward. This process took place over a long period of time. The high peaks and ridges that were finally thrust above the surface of the water formed the islands of Japan.

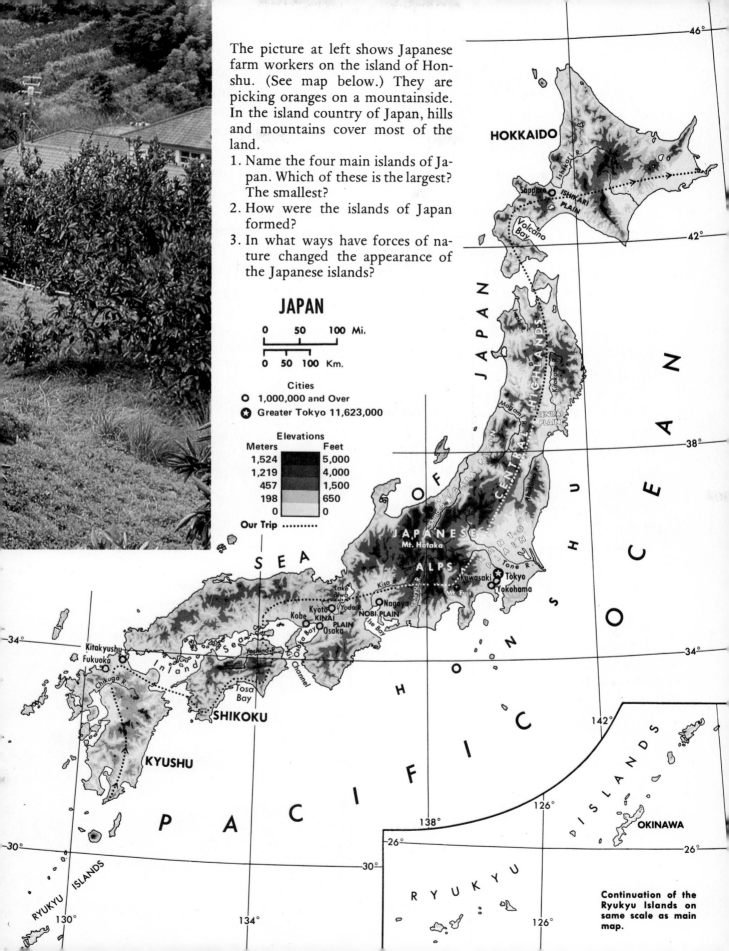

The picture at left shows Japanese farm workers on the island of Honshu. (See map below.) They are picking oranges on a mountainside. In the island country of Japan, hills and mountains cover most of the land.

1. Name the four main islands of Japan. Which of these is the largest? The smallest?
2. How were the islands of Japan formed?
3. In what ways have forces of nature changed the appearance of the Japanese islands?

JAPAN

0   50   100 Mi.

0   50 100 Km.

Cities
◯ 1,000,000 and Over
✪ Greater Tokyo 11,623,000

Elevations

Meters		Feet
1,524		5,000
1,219		4,000
457		1,500
198		650
0		0

Our Trip ··········

HOKKAIDO

Sapporo ISHKARI PLAIN

Ishkari R.

Volcano Bay

SEA

OF

JAPAN

CENTRAL HIGHLANDS

Mogami R.

Kitakami R.

SENDAI PLAIN

NIIGATA PLAIN

Shinano R.

JAPANESE
Mt. Hotaka
ALPS

KANTO PLAIN

Kiso R.

Tone R.

Lake Biwa

Yodo R.

Nagoya

NOBI PLAIN

Kyoto

Kobe KINAI PLAIN
Osaka

Ise Bay

Mt. Fuji

Kawasaki Tokyo
Yokohama

Osaka Bay

Inland Sea

Yoshino R.

Bungo Channel

Tosa Bay

SHIKOKU

Kitakyushu
Fukuoka

Chikugo R.

KYUSHU

HONSHU

PACIFIC   OCEAN

RYUKYU ISLANDS

OKINAWA

Continuation of the Ryukyu Islands on same scale as main map.

46°

42°

38°

34°

34°

30°

26°

26°

130°   134°   138°   142°   126°   126°

Over the centuries, powerful forces of nature changed the appearance of the Japanese islands. Earthquakes forced some parts of the islands to rise and others to sink. Volcanoes erupted in some places and piled up masses of lava and ashes, forming new mountains. These high, cone-shaped mountains still stand in sharp contrast to the jagged peaks around them. Swift mountain streams washed soil and loose rock down the mountain slopes and deposited this material in valleys and along the coasts. These areas became filled in with rock and soil, forming the fertile plains on which most of Japan's people live today.

Nature is still changing this rugged, beautiful country. There are earthquakes every day, but most of these are too slight to notice. About fifty of Japan's volcanoes are still active. At times, some of them send showers of ashes or streams of molten lava down on the surrounding countryside.

A tour of Japan. One of the best ways to see what the land of Japan looks like today is to tour the country by helicopter. The map on page 25 suggests one route for such a tour.

A Problem To Solve
The picture at right was taken on an island in Japan's Inland Sea. How do land and water features affect the lives of Japan's people? In forming hypotheses to solve this problem, you will need to consider facts about the following:
1. population distribution in Japan
2. ways in which the Japanese earn their living
3. trade and transportation within Japan and between Japan and other parts of the world
4. leisure-time activities in Japan
Other chapters provide additional information that will be helpful in solving this problem.

Kyushu. Your tour begins on the island of Kyushu, in the far southwestern part of Japan. Much of the land in the southern part of this island is a rolling plateau,* formed of volcanic ash and lava. When you reach central Kyushu, however, you see many steep, forested mountains. In the northern part of the island, your helicopter crosses low hills and wide plains. There are many cities here, for this is one of the main manufacturing areas in Japan.

*See Glossary

Shikoku. East of Kyushu you come to the island of Shikoku. The coast here is very rocky. Fishing villages are built along the narrow strips of beach. Farther inland, the land is covered with rugged ridges and narrow valleys. As you fly along the southern coast of Shikoku, you notice that the shoreline curves inward. Inside this curve are the blue waters of Tosa Bay. (See map on page 25.) A narrow plain borders the bay. From Tosa Bay, you fly across densely forested mountains to the northern coast of Shikoku. Here the land slopes gently downward to the Inland Sea. There are many rice fields in this fertile coastal area. A number of industrial cities are located here, also.

The Inland Sea. Leaving Shikoku you fly north across the beautiful Inland Sea. (See map on page 25.) This sheltered waterway is bordered by three of Japan's largest islands. From your helicopter you notice that the Inland Sea

Mount Fuji, Japan's highest mountain peak, is located on the island of Honshu. Hills and towering mountains cover much of the land on Honshu, but there are lowlands along the coasts.

is dotted with hundreds of smaller islands. In little coves along the shores of these hilly, forested islands are many farming and fishing villages.

Honshu. You are now over the southern coast of Honshu, Japan's largest and most important island. On the small lowlands along the coast are many farms, towns, and cities. Farther inland, the land becomes more rugged. Forests grow on the higher, steeper slopes here. On the lower slopes and in the valleys are fields of crops.

Now your helicopter heads eastward, across Honshu. Below is Lake Biwa, Japan's largest lake. (See map on page 25.) Ahead are the towering peaks of the Japanese Alps, the highest mountain range in Japan. There are many volcanoes in this range.

You continue eastward to another line of volcanoes, which includes Mount Fuji, the most famous mountain

in Japan. (See picture on opposite page.) Fuji is the highest single mountain peak in Japan. It rises 12,389 feet above sea level. Your helicopter lands for a while at the edge of the huge crater at Fuji's summit. From the pilot you learn that the last time this volcano erupted was in 1707.

Northeast of Mount Fuji is the Kanto Plain, Japan's largest lowland. (See map on page 25.) On this plain are large industrial cities and fertile rice fields.

Soon you board your helicopter again and fly north. Three chains of highlands stretch side by side through the part of Honshu you are now crossing. The central chain is higher than the ones on either side. West of the highlands is the Niigata Plain with its wide, green rice fields. It is bordered by sand dunes along the sea. Farther north, and east of the highlands, is the Sendai Plain.

Hokkaido. You continue northward to Hokkaido, which is Japan's second largest island. Jutting out from the southwestern corner of this island is a hilly, hook-shaped peninsula. Inside the hook lies Volcano Bay. To the northeast is the Ishikari Plain. Other plains lie along the southern and eastern coasts of the island. Forested mountains cover much of the rest of the land.

As you cross Hokkaido, you notice that it differs from the other islands of Japan in several ways. There are fewer cities here, and the farms are larger. The map on page 69 shows that Hokkaido is the most thinly populated of the four main islands in Japan. One reason why few people have settled on Hokkaido is that the winters here are very cold and long. As you will discover in Chapter 13, the severe winters cause farming in Hokkaido to differ from farming in other parts of Japan.

A farm on Hokkaido. What are some ways Hokkaido differs from the other islands of Japan?

2 Climate

A country with changing seasons and plentiful rainfall. The climate of Japan is somewhat like the climate of the Atlantic coast of the United States. Japan stretches many miles from north to south and is much cooler in the north than in the south. It also has changing seasons. In addition, Japan receives plentiful rainfall. More rain falls in summer than in winter. To learn more about the climate of Japan and its effects, we will describe the four seasons of the year in this beautiful island country.

<u>Winter.</u> It is December in Japan. On the island of Hokkaido and along the northwestern coast of Honshu, the ground is blanketed with heavy snow. Roads are sometimes blocked for days at a time. The skies are cloudy, and the air is damp and cold.

Winds from the northwest bring this weather to northwestern Japan. These winds are called the winter monsoons.* They begin in the cold interior of northern Asia. At the beginning of their journey these winds are icy cold and very dry. As they cross the Sea of Japan, however, they are warmed enough to absorb some moisture. As these winds rise to cross the

*See Glossary

Physical Needs

See pages 76-77

The skiers shown in the picture at right are enjoying fresh air and sunshine in the Japanese Alps. Discuss the following questions with other students in your class.
1. Do you think everyone has a need for physical activity? Give reasons for your answer.
2. What do you think would happen to a person who couldn't get any exercise? Explain.
3. How do you meet your need for exercise?

mountains in northwestern Japan, they lose much of their moisture in the form of snow.

In southeastern Japan, winter days are very different. Although the air is cold everywhere except in the southernmost part of the country, the sky is clear and sunny. Very little rain or snow falls here during the winter. In some places, farmers work in their wheat and barley fields at this time of the year.

There are several reasons why winters are milder and less snowy in southeastern Japan. Mountains shelter this part of the country from some of the cold winter monsoons. The winds that do cross the mountains bring little snow, for they have already lost much of their moisture. Also, this part of the country is closer to the equator.

Spring. Now it is a cool, clear day in March. Big white clouds float lazily in the sky. Winter snows have melted, except in the mountains and in the far north. Spring is coming to Japan.

During April, the weather is often sunny and warm. Throughout much of the country, fields and hillsides are bright with flowers. The smell of pink cherry blossoms fills the air. Spring is a beautiful time of year in Japan.

Summer. The month of June is here now, and the skies are cloudy. Except

A crowded beach at Kanazawa, on the Sea of Japan. In summer, many people enjoy visiting the beaches along Japan's coasts. A warm ocean current bathes the shores of southern and central Japan. It helps to make summers hot and humid in much of the country.

TYPHOONS

During the late summer and early fall, the skies in southern Japan are sometimes darkened by fierce storms. These storms are like the hurricanes that sometimes strike the southeastern coast of the United States. In the western Pacific, they are called typhoons.

Hurricanes and typhoons are the most destructive storms known. They are made up of violent winds that whirl around a calm center called the eye. The eye is usually about fifteen miles in diameter, but the entire storm may be as much as five hundred miles across. Such a storm is not considered a true hurricane or typhoon unless the whirling winds near the center blow at a speed of seventy-five miles an hour or more. The storm itself, however, travels rather slowly, at about fifteen or twenty miles an hour.

Hurricanes and typhoons form in the tropics, over large bodies of warm water. North of the equator, where these storms are most frequent, they travel northwestward until they reach about 25° or 30° north latitude. Then they may change direction and move northeastward. South of the equator, hurricanes and typhoons move southwestward and then southeastward. The map below shows where these storms are most frequently formed, and the directions they generally follow.

Usually, several typhoons form over the Pacific Ocean each year. Some of these storms remain over the ocean. Others, however, move toward land, striking such areas as southern Japan, the Philippines, and the coast of mainland Asia. The violent winds of a typhoon often cause great destruction of property. Sometimes many people are killed. The enormous tidal waves and heavy rains that come with typhoons may also cause damage. Fortunately, typhoons seldom reach far inland.

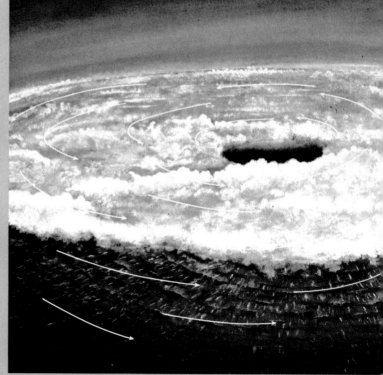

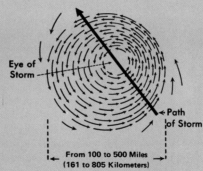

ROTATION OF WINDS IN A TYPHOON

Eye of Storm

Path of Storm

From 100 to 500 Miles
(161 to 805 Kilometers)

A typhoon is made up of violent winds that whirl around a calm center called the eye. (See illustration above.) In the Northern Hemisphere, the whirling winds of typhoons and other circular storms blow in a counter-clockwise direction. (See chart at left.) In the Southern Hemisphere, they blow in a clockwise direction.

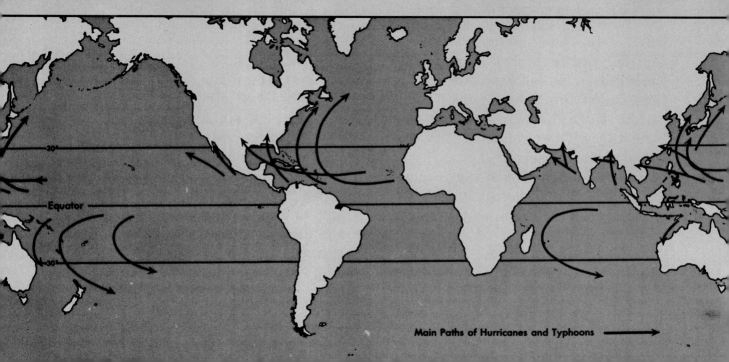

Equator

Main Paths of Hurricanes and Typhoons ⟶

The picture above shows people in Kyoto on a rainy day. In Japan, the average yearly rainfall differs considerably from place to place. (See map on opposite page.)

on the northernmost island of Japan, drizzling rains fall day after day. They are called the "plum rains," for they occur when the plums are ripening on the trees. These rains are very important to the farmers of Japan. They provide water to irrigate the fields in which rice, Japan's main crop, is grown. (See Chapter 13.)

It is now the end of July, and the plum rains have ended. Although the days are usually clear, the weather in much of Japan is hot and sticky. Even

at night the air is moist and uncomfortable. Many vacationers crowd the sandy beaches along the coasts. Some go north to Hokkaido, for summers are cooler in that part of the country.

Summer monsoons from the southeast help to cause the kind of weather Japan has during this season. The summer monsoons that blow to southern and central Japan cross a warm ocean current called the Japan Current. (See map on opposite page.) This current warms the monsoons that cross it and

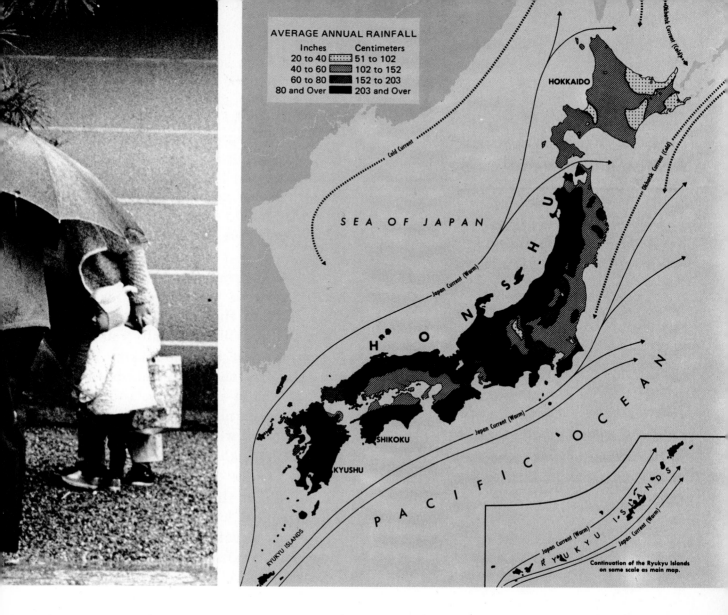

makes them very damp. As a result, they help to bring hot, humid summer weather to southern and central Japan. However, the summer monsoons that blow to northern Japan cross the cold Okhotsk Current* on their way. As they do so, they are chilled, and help to keep summers in northern Japan cooler than they might be otherwise. Beginning in late summer, destructive storms called typhoons sometimes strike Japan.

<u>Fall</u>. Rice fields are turning yellow now, for it is autumn in Japan. The leaves of the maple and oak trees are changing from green to vivid shades of red and gold. Most of the days are pleasant and sunny, but there is a chill in the air. Soon the cold days of winter will be here again.

Climate in the mountains. The climate just described is found in the lowlands of Japan. To show what the climate is like in the mountainous regions of the country, we will describe a hike up Mount Hotaka, in the Japanese Alps. (See map on page 25.)

Hikers in the mountains. Summer weather is cooler in the mountains of Japan than in near-by lowlands. Explain why this is so.

It is a warm summer day. The path you follow in the foothills of the mountain leads through a dense forest of aspen and elm trees. At the beginning of the hike the sun feels very hot. Halfway up the mountainside, however, you notice that the air feels cooler and crisper. There are no aspen and elm trees this far up the mountainside. Instead, the slopes are covered with pine trees.

As you continue to climb, the air becomes colder. Only short grass and moss cling to the rocky slopes. Snow lies in shaded hollows. Finally you reach the summit of the mountain. Here, more than ten thousand feet above sea level, it is cold and sunny, and sharp winds blow. On all sides you see massive peaks, spotted with snow. If summer is so cool this high above sea level, you can imagine how cold winter must be.

Let's explore the reasons why the air high above sea level is colder than the air at lower elevations. As you probably know, air is warmed by the heat that the earth receives from the sun. At low elevations, much of this heat is absorbed by the molecules of oxygen, nitrogen, and other gases that make up the air. Heat is also absorbed by moisture and particles of dust in the air. For these reasons, air at low elevations is relatively warm. At high elevations, however, the air is much thinner; there are not enough molecules of gases to absorb much heat. Also, the air at high levels contains less moisture and fewer dust particles to absorb heat. Thus, temperatures are almost always cooler at higher elevations. Each three to four hundred feet of elevation makes a difference of one degree in temperature.

Make a Relief Map

With a group of your classmates, make a relief map of Japan. To carry out this project, follow these steps.

1. Trace the country's outline from a large map of Japan. Use carbon paper to transfer this outline to a piece of heavy cardboard.
2. Using the map on page 25 as a guide, form the various land elevations of Japan with papier-mâché.
3. After allowing the papier-mâché to dry thoroughly (at least twenty-four hours), paint your relief map with poster paints or tempera. You may wish to use brown for the high mountains, green for the lowlands, and yellow for the areas of medium elevation. You might use blue paint to show major rivers and waters that border Japan.

The suggestions on page 175, in the Skills Manual, will be helpful in making your map.

Our Changing Earth

For billions of years, nature has been in the process of creating the earth's varied land and water features. Do research to discover ways in which changes in the earth's surface are brought about. You may wish to write a report about your discoveries in which you explain how each of the following affects the earth's surface:

a. earthquakes
b. volcanoes
c. weathering
d. erosion
e. continental drift

The suggestions on pages 177-182 will help you find information and write a good report.

The Pacific Ring of Fire

Earthquakes and volcanoes are common in Japan and other lands that border the Pacific Ocean. These lands form a rough circle, which is often referred to as the Pacific ring of fire. Draw a map of the Pacific Ocean and the lands that border it. Then do research to discover where the most frequent earthquakes in these lands occur, and the location of active volcanoes. Mark these places on your map, using appropriate symbols. When your map is completed, display it in your classroom.

Investigate Two Ocean Currents

Two ocean currents help to determine the climate of Japan. One of these is the Japan Current. The other is the Okhotsk Current, which is also called the Oyashio. Do research in this book and other sources to discover answers to the following questions.

1. What is an ocean current?
2. Where does the Japan Current begin? Where does it flow?
3. Is the Japan Current warm or cold?
4. Why is the Japan Current sometimes called "the Gulf Stream of the Pacific"?
5. How does the Japan Current affect the climate of Japan?
6. Where does the Okhotsk Current flow?
7. Is the Okhotsk Current warm or cold?
8. How does the Okhotsk Current influence the climate of Japan?

When you have completed your research, you may wish to share your findings with your classmates by presenting a brief oral report. See the suggestions on pages 180-182, in the Skills Manual.

Make Comparisons

You know that one of the most important influences on the climate of any place in the world is its distance from the equator. However, as you have learned from the Climate chapter, there are other important influences on climate. If you will look at a globe or a world map, you will find that the island of Hokkaido is about the same distance from the equator as Mongolia, the Black Sea coast of the Soviet Union, the province of Nova Scotia in Canada, and the state of Washington in the United States. Use encyclopedias and other books to learn about the climate of these different places. Then try to answer the following questions.

1. In what ways, if any, are the climates of these places alike?
2. In what ways, if any, are the climates of these places different? What are some reasons for these differences?

Discuss these questions with your classmates. Suggestions for holding a group discussion are given on pages 182-183, in the Skills Manual.

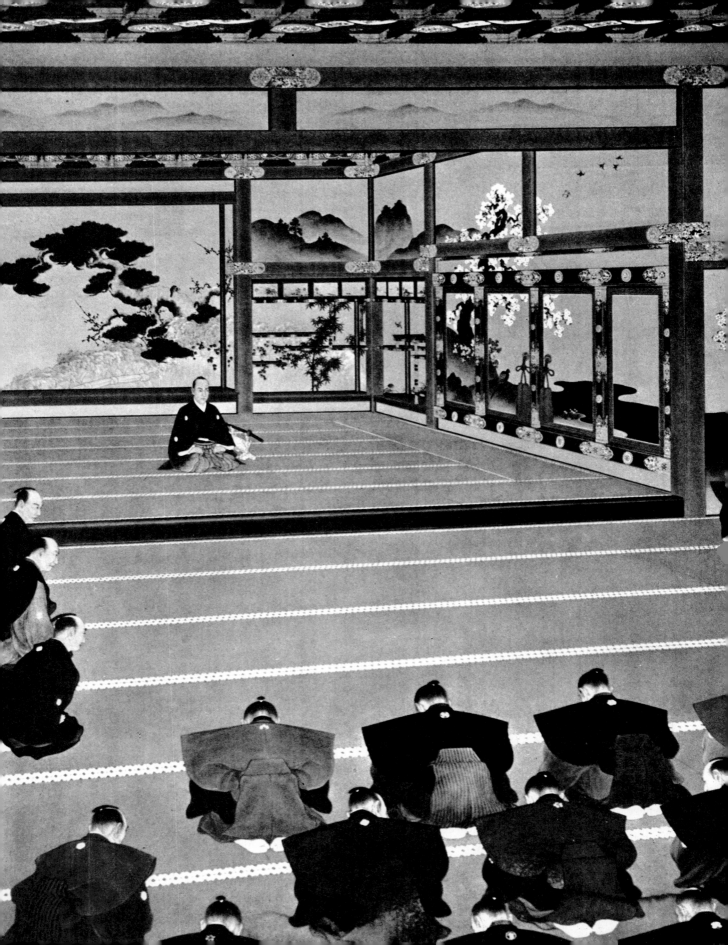

Part 2
History and Government

Japan is a very old country. As you do research about this country's history and government in the chapters in Part 2, you may wish to consider the following questions.

- What are some ways in which Japan has changed through the years?
- What are some ways in which Japan has maintained old traditions?
- Who do you think were some of the most important persons in Japan's history? Give reasons for your choices.
- What kind of government does Japan have today?
- How long has Japan had this kind of government?
- Do you think a study of Japan's history can help you understand life in Japan today? Give reasons for thinking as you do.

If you wish to do additional research in other sources, refer to the suggestions on pages 177-179, in the Skills Manual. The projects suggested on page 65 will also help you to make interesting discoveries about Japan's history.

Change and Continuity

From 1603 to 1867, Japan was ruled by a series of dictators known as the Tokugawa shoguns. The picture at left shows the last of these shoguns announcing, in 1867, that he will give up his power to the emperor of Japan. What does the word "shogun" mean? How did the Tokugawa shoguns come to power? How were they able to stay in control of Japan for such a long period? What changes in Japan finally led to the overthrow of the Tokugawa shoguns? Do research in Chapter 3 to discover answers to these questions.

3 From Ancient to Modern Times

The early people of Japan. No one knows for certain when people first came to the islands of Japan. At the time Christ was born, however, the ancestors of the present-day Japanese were living in the southern part of the islands. Primitive people called the Ainu were living in the rest of Japan. (See picture at right.) The Japanese were gradually moving northward, taking over by force the lands that belonged to the Ainu.

The types of houses the early Japanese built, and the legends they have passed down are like those of people in several other parts of Asia. For these and other reasons, scholars believe that the early Japanese were descended from various groups of people who had come to the islands from other parts of Asia. Most of these people seem to have come from northern and eastern Asia by way of the peninsula of Korea. (See map on pages 6 and 7.) Some probably came from lands farther to the south.

In the early centuries of the Christian Era, the Japanese were divided into independent clans.* The clans often fought each other for land and power. One of them, the Yamato clan, was more powerful than the rest. As time went on the Yamato chief came to be recognized as the leader of the other clan chiefs.

The early Japanese had a very simple way of life. They made their homes in villages, and farmed and fished for food. Rice was their main crop. These early people did not know how to read or write. The weapons and tools they used were very crude.

The religion of the early Japanese was a form of nature worship later called Shinto. (See pages 73 and 75.) Each of the clan chiefs claimed to be descended from one of the Shinto gods. The chief of the Yamato clan claimed that the Sun Goddess, the most important Shinto deity, was his ancestor.

The Japanese learn from the Chinese. Across the sea from the islands of Japan is China. At the time when life in

*See Glossary

Ainu people wearing their traditional costumes. They are descendants of early people who once occupied much of Japan. Many centuries ago, the Ainu were pushed northward by the ancestors of the present-day Japanese people. Today, most Ainu live on Hokkaido.

Japan was still quite primitive, China was already a great empire with a strong central government headed by an emperor. The Chinese had produced great art, literature, and philosophy. They also had learned how to construct beautiful buildings, to make tools of iron, and to weave cloth of silk.

Early in their history, the Japanese began to borrow Chinese ideas. Until the end of the sixth century A.D., most of these ideas came secondhand from the people of Korea, who lived near China. During these early centuries, the

Chinese form of writing and the Buddhist* religion were brought to Japan. The Japanese also learned to weave silk and to make articles of metal.

In the seventh century A.D., Japanese students and observers went directly to China. They were sent by leaders of the Yamato clan to study the laws, government, and political ideas of the Chinese. These ideas helped the Yamato leaders in Japan to establish a central government, which was headed by an emperor. By the end of the seventh century, the leaders of the other clans had been brought under the control of this central government.

Although the Japanese borrowed a great deal from the Chinese, they did not copy them exactly. The Japanese chose only what they wanted and shaped it to fit their own needs.

Landowning warriors become powerful, and the country is torn by warfare. The central government that was established in Japan during the seventh century did not remain strong very long. In the following centuries, government officials, living in luxury in the capital city, became careless and weak. As the power of the central government grew weaker, a number of landowning families began to grow very powerful. The warrior chieftains of these families ruled all who lived on their lands. They hired soldiers to defend their lands and fight against their rivals. The soldiers came to be called samurai.

Like the clan leaders of early Japan, the landowning chieftains fought each other frequently. In 1185, one power-

Japanese warriors in the twelfth century. For hundreds of years, Japan was torn by civil wars.

ful chieftain named Yoritomo defeated his principal rival. In 1192, the emperor gave to Yoritomo the title "shogun," which means "general."

Shogun Yoritomo set up a military government of his own. He permitted the emperor to remain on the throne. However, the shogun's government was now the real power in Japan. For almost seven hundred years after this, Japan was ruled by shoguns.

Japan continued to be torn by wars. In the thirteenth century, people called Mongols, from central Asia, tried to invade the Japanese islands, but they failed. About fifty years later the emperor unsuccessfully struggled with the shogun for control of Japan. In the centuries that followed, the leaders of rival landowning families frequently fought each other for the powerful position of shogun. These civil wars caused much destruction.

Three great warriors bring peace to Japan. Early in the seventeenth century, the civil wars in Japan ended. Three

What caused these destructive conflicts? When and how did the civil wars finally come to an end?

Loyalty

See page 164

Tokugawa Ieyasu became shogun of Japan in 1603. He and the shoguns who followed him demanded unquestioning loyalty from the Japanese people.

1. Why do you think these rulers demanded such strict loyalty? Do you think it was good for Japan? Explain your answer.
2. Why did the Tokugawas force European missionaries to leave Japan?
3. Do you believe people in our country should show unquestioning loyalty toward the government? Why? Why not?

great warriors had a part in bringing about this peace. The first was a land-owning warrior named Nobunaga. Between 1560 and 1582, this great warrior brought most of Japan under his control. Nobunaga was killed in 1582, but the military unification of the country was completed by one of his generals, Hideyoshi. After Hideyoshi's death, rebellion broke out again, but the country was soon brought firmly under the control of his ally Tokugawa Ieyasu.

Japan becomes a dictatorship isolated from the rest of the world. Tokugawa Ieyasu became shogun of Japan in 1603. From that time until 1867, Japan was ruled by shoguns of the Tokugawa family. During most of this period, the country was at peace.

How were the Tokugawas able to stay in power so long? One reason is that they set up a dictatorship under which it was almost impossible for people to revolt. The emperor was kept under close watch to make certain he did not plot a rebellion. Strict laws also were made to keep rival landowners from rebelling. These landowners were required to have homes in Edo, the Tokugawa capital, as well as on their own lands. When they were not at the capital, they had to leave their families there as hostages. In addition, they had to spend large sums of money building temples, roads, and other public works. As a result, the landowners could not save enough money to use for a revolt against the Tokugawas. To make certain no one secretly tried to rebel, the Tokugawas had many spies.

The Tokugawas tried to prevent changes from taking place in Japan that would endanger their power. People were strictly divided into four classes. The highest class was made up of the military — landowning warriors and their private armies. Beneath this warrior class were the farmer, craft worker, and merchant classes. Rules were made stating what kind of clothes people should wear, what kind of houses they should build, and how they should behave. A person who tried to be different could be severely punished. Unquestioning obedience and loyalty to those in authority were considered the highest virtues.

The Tokugawas were especially worried about the influence of European traders and missionaries in Japan. These people had begun coming to Japan during the 1500's. There was the danger that rival landowners in distant parts of Japan might become wealthy and powerful if they were allowed to trade with foreigners. In addition, the Christian religion which the missionaries had introduced, taught that every person's final loyalty should be to God, not to the government.

To guard against these and other possible dangers, the Tokugawas decided to close Japan off from the rest of the world. At first, only foreign missionaries were forced to leave. By the middle of the 1600's, however, most foreign traders were made to leave also. After that time, no foreigners except a few Dutch and Chinese traders were permitted to come to Japan. These few traders were allowed to come only to the small port of Nagasaki in western Kyushu. The Tokugawa leaders did not permit Japanese traders to go to other countries, either. They did not even allow Japanese who were living in other countries to return home.

Japan lived apart from the world for more than two centuries. During this time, farming methods improved, and many people developed great skills as artists and craft workers. Living together under the firm rule of the Tokugawas, the Japanese came to have a strong feeling of belonging together as a nation.

Japan begins to change. The laws made by the Tokugawa rulers could not stop change from coming to Japan. During the years of peace, towns and cities grew up near the castles of the warrior landowners, and the Tokugawa capital, Edo, became a great city. Also, more and more people began to use money to buy the things they needed, instead of exchanging goods with one another. Soon, money became important as a means of trade.

Many people in Japan become discontented with their Tokugawa leaders. The growing use of money helped many Japanese merchants who bought and sold goods to become wealthy. In spite of their wealth, however, the merchants were considered to belong to the lower classes of people, and were not permitted to do many things they wanted. This turned many of them against the Tokugawa leaders.

Landowners and farm workers in Japan were discontented also. As you learned earlier, the Tokugawa leaders forced the landowners to build roads and other public works, and to have homes in the capital city as well as on their own lands. Many landowners had to borrow money from the wealthy merchants to pay for these expensive projects. To obtain money to pay their debts, the landowners made the farmers on their land pay higher taxes. As time went on, both the farmers and the landowners became increasingly poor and dissatisfied with their Tokugawa leaders.

There were also some scholars in Japan who were discontented. Among these were students of Japanese history and philosophy who felt that the emperor, not the Tokugawa shogun, was the rightful ruler of Japan. Others were scholars who had learned about the United States and the countries of Europe through the small group of Dutch traders who were allowed to come to Japan. These scholars had first learned the Dutch language and then studied Dutch books on subjects such as science, engineering, and medicine. They realized that the Western* countries were rapidly developing into industrial powers. Some of these scholars felt that Japan should open its ports for world trade and become more modern. Otherwise, they felt Japan would be conquered by these stronger Western nations.

Foreign nations want to trade with Japan. In addition to discontent inside Japan, the Tokugawa rulers faced problems from outside during the nineteenth century. Foreign nations were asking the Japanese to open their ports for trade. For a time, the Tokugawa rulers refused these requests. In the summer of 1853, however, four American warships under the command of Commodore Perry sailed into Edo Bay, now called Tokyo Bay. Commodore

Perry had been sent to open friendly relations between the United States and Japan. The United States wanted Japan to open a few ports for trade, to allow American ships to buy fuel in Japan, and to protect American sailors who were shipwrecked on Japanese shores.

Exchange

See page 164

In 1853, American warships commanded by Commodore Matthew C. Perry sailed into what is now called Tokyo Bay. The picture above shows Perry meeting with Japanese officials. He gave them a letter from the President of the United States, asking for trading privileges and other rights. In following years, Japan made trade agreements with the United States and other countries. Why had the Tokugawa shoguns previously restricted trade with foreign nations? Do you think the establishment of trade relations with other countries affected Japan's history? Give reasons for your answer.

47

When the Tokugawa leaders saw Perry's ships, they became confused and afraid. They knew that their own small boats would be useless against these great steamships that moved against the wind. They also knew that their firearms were no match for the great guns mounted on the ships.

Japan opens to the world. The Tokugawa leaders did not want to grant Perry's request, but they finally came to realize they had no choice. In 1854, Japan signed a treaty opening two ports to American ships. As the years passed, more treaties were signed with the United States and other countries. These treaties caused much discontent in Japan, for there were many Japanese who did not want their country to give up its position of isolation. However, by the 1870's, resistance to opening the country had been broken.

The emperor becomes the real ruler of Japan. The changes that took place in Japan during the nineteenth century made people in Japan realize that the Tokugawa rulers were no longer as powerful as before. Many Japanese decided to help the emperor's government overthrow the Tokugawa government. For a number of years, there was strife between the supporters of the emperor and those of the Tokugawa shogun. Finally the shogun came to see that his struggle to stay in power was hopeless. In 1867, he announced that he was willing to permit the emperor to become Japan's real ruler.

Japan becomes a modern country. The Japanese have a custom of giving a special name to the period of time that each Japanese emperor rules. "Meiji" was the name given to the reign of the emperor who came to power after the Tokugawa shogun. The name Meiji means "enlightened rule." It is a good name for this reign, as the emperor and his advisors were intelligent, practical leaders, who ruled wisely and well.

At the time Emperor Meiji came to power, European nations were taking over large parts of Asia. The emperor's advisors realized that if Japan remained a farming country, it would soon be taken over also. To prevent this from happening, they set to work to modernize their country. Like the leaders of the Yamato clan in the seventh century, the Meiji leaders sent Japanese students and observers abroad to learn from more advanced countries. The Meiji government also invited industrial, military, communication, and transportation advisors from Europe and the United States to come to Japan.

Japan's government is modernized. The Meiji leaders knew that one of Japan's important needs was to have a strong central government to which all the people would feel loyal. Under the shoguns, the great landowners had governed the people who lived on their lands. Under the Meiji leaders the governing powers of the landowners were taken over by the central government. A constitution was written outlining how the government should be run, and a lawmaking assembly called the Diet was formed. The new government was not democratic, for there was nothing in Japan's history to prepare its leaders or citizens for democracy. The constitution stated that the emperor was a sacred person whose actions

Emperor Meiji gained control of Japan's government after the Tokugawa shogun gave up his position in 1867. What does the name Meiji mean? Give several examples to support the belief that Meiji is a good name for this emperor's reign.

could not be questioned, and the Diet was given no real power. The government was very efficient, however, and was greatly respected by the people.

The armed forces are modernized. The Meiji leaders also felt that Japan needed to have a modern army in order to protect its independence. Under the

Tokugawas, only the warrior class, made up of landowners and their private armies, had been allowed to carry weapons. The Meiji leaders dismissed the samurai and established a national army made up of soldiers drafted from all classes of people. A modern navy was established, also.

Modern industries are started. Weapons were needed for Japan's new army. The Meiji leaders knew that Japan would not be able to arm itself unless it became a modern industrial nation with steel mills, shipyards, and railroads. The first industries and transportation facilities in Japan were established mainly by the government. However, the government also encouraged private industry. By the beginning of the twentieth century, Japan was on the way to becoming an important manufacturing country.

Education is modernized. The Meiji leaders also realized that Japan could not become a modern nation unless its people had the skills and the education they needed to live in the modern world. In 1872, a public school system was started. By 1900, Japan also had its own job-training and teacher-training schools.

Why was Japan able to become a modern nation with so little difficulty? The period of time from the opening of Japan's ports until the death of the Meiji emperor in 1912 was only about half a century. During this time, Japan changed from a farming nation to one of the world's important industrial countries. This amazing progress can be understood better when you review Japan's history. The Japanese had become a highly civilized nation long before their country closed itself off from the world. After Japan closed its ports, the Japanese had two centuries of peace in which to develop their skills still further. Living close together on their islands, they came to feel that they were different from other nations, and proud that they were Japanese. Also, during these two centuries, the ideas of loyalty and unquestioning obedience to those in authority became firmly established. It is no wonder that once the highly civilized, well-disciplined Japanese people received the education they needed for life in the modern world, they were able to make such amazing progress.

Prince Iwakura and other Japanese officials leaving Yokohama Harbor on a trip to the United States and Europe, in 1871. The Meiji leaders sent many people abroad in the late 1800's. What do you suppose the Japanese wanted to learn from foreign nations?

4 From Empire to Democracy

A Problem To Solve

After the Japanese opened their doors to the world, they set out to conquer other lands and establish an empire. Why did the Japanese want an empire? In forming your hypotheses, you will need to think about the following factors:

a. the actions of European nations at the time Japan opened its ports for trade
b. Japan's need for food, raw materials, and places to sell its manufactured goods
c. the position that the warrior class held in Japan in earlier times   See Skills Manual, pages 166–169

Japan becomes a world power. During the years that Japan was changing to an industrial nation, it also was establishing an empire. In two wars, one with China and one with Russia, the Japanese gained Formosa,* several other islands in the Pacific, and valuable territories in Manchuria.* In 1910, Korea also became a Japanese possession. At the end of World War I,* Japan was awarded control over some very important islands in the Pacific that had belonged to Germany. By 1919, Japan was recognized as one of the world's leading powers.

Why did the Japanese want to conquer lands outside their own islands? There were many reasons why the Japanese wanted additional territory. Powerful European nations were taking over large parts of Asia at the time the Japanese opened their ports for trade. Japan wanted to establish an empire partly to protect itself from these European con-

*See Glossary

52

querors, and partly to prove that it was powerful, too.

Chapter 12 helps to explain another reason why the Japanese wanted an empire. Japan is a crowded country with little farmland and not enough natural resources for industry. The only way it can provide its people with a good standard of living is by selling manufactured goods to other countries and by using the money earned this way to import food and raw materials. Like other powerful nations, Japan thought it needed an empire in order to have a place to sell its manufactured goods and to obtain raw materials and food.

There was still another reason why Japan wanted to conquer other territories. As Chapter 3 explains, there has been much warfare in Japan's past, and military leaders have always been considered very important. After Japan opened its ports and began to modernize its country, many officers in its new army and navy continued to be interested in war. They believed in force and felt that Japan had the right to conquer other countries. There were some people in Japan who realized this was a foolish ambition. However, a majority of Japanese listened to the military leaders with great respect.

Conflict

The Battle of the Japan Sea, during the Russo-Japanese War (1904-1905). In the early part of the twentieth century, Japan was involved in several wars. How did these conflicts help Japan become a world power?

Military leaders gain control of Japan.
In the 1930's, the leaders of Japan's army and navy were able to gain control of the government. The military leaders took advantage of the people's feeling of patriotism to win support. They emphasized that the emperor was a god, saying that the world should be united under his divine rule. They also told the people that the way to show loyalty to the emperor was through obedience to the military leaders who represented him. Newspapers and radio programs were used to plant this idea firmly in the people's minds.

Force also was used to bring the military leaders to power. Many influential people who opposed the militarists were murdered. Some of these murders were done by army officers. Others were done by groups of people who supported the militarists. As time went on, fewer and fewer Japanese dared speak out against the nation's military leaders.

The ambitions of Japan's militarists lead the country into war. As you learned earlier, Japan's militarists wanted to conquer other nations. In 1931, against the will of several government leaders, Japanese troops began to take over Manchuria, in northeastern China. In 1933, the Japanese troops marched farther into China. For a time, the Chinese did little to resist. However, Japan's troops advanced deeper into the heart of China in 1937, and the two countries went to war. The Chinese were badly mistreated by the Japanese troops who invaded their homeland.

Countries in other parts of the world disapproved of Japan's actions. The United States was especially disturbed,

because in 1900, it had declared an "open door" policy for China. This policy was intended to keep China independent and open to traders from all nations. Neither the United States nor any other country tried to stop Japan,

however, for they did not want to risk going to war themselves.

The next warlike action of the Japanese military leaders was encouraged by events in a distant part of the world. In 1939 and 1940, the European country of Germany invaded several neighboring countries, leading western Europe

Japanese troops in China. In the 1930's military leaders who felt it was Japan's right and duty to conquer other nations gained control of the Japanese government. Japanese troops advanced deep into the heart of China during this decade, and the two countries went to war.

-2

The Japanese attacked the United States naval base at Pearl Harbor on December 7, 1941, bringing both nations into World War II (left). On August 14, 1945, Japan agreed to surrender. The surrender papers were signed September 2 aboard the United States warship *Missouri* (right).

into World War II. Japan's leaders decided to take advantage of this situation. In 1940 they began moving troops into Indochina,* a French territory. It soon became clear that Japan intended to take over all of eastern Asia.

In 1941, the United States and several European countries finally decided to take strong action to show their disapproval of Japan. Almost all shipments of goods to Japan were stopped. Japan's answer to this action was not long in coming. On December 7, 1941, Japanese airplanes bombed the United States naval base at Pearl Harbor in Hawaii. The next day the United States declared war on Japan. This brought both countries into World War II.

From glory to defeat. When the Japanese entered World War II, no country was prepared to oppose them. The United States Navy had suffered heavy losses of ships and planes at Pearl Harbor. Japanese troops were able to advance very swiftly. By the middle of 1942, Japan had conquered almost all of southeastern Asia and the southwest Pacific.

Japan's time of glory did not last long, however. By the end of 1942, the United States was ready to fight back. During the months that followed, Japan met defeat after defeat on land, at sea, and in the air. By the summer of 1945, American warships were off the coast of Japan, and American airplanes

General Douglas MacArthur (at the microphone) led the forces that occupied Japan after the war. What were some accomplishments of the Occupation?

1945, atomic bombs were dropped on the cities of Hiroshima and Nagasaki. Both cities were severely damaged and thousands of people were killed.

Now the Japanese had to make a decision. Some military leaders wanted to go on with the war, preferring death to surrender. Civilian leaders realized that continuing the war would mean the total destruction of Japan. The emperor of Japan listened to both sides in silence. Then he made the decision. Japan must admit defeat. On September 2, 1945, representatives of the Japanese government signed surrender papers aboard the United States warship *Missouri*. General Douglas MacArthur, Supreme Commander for the Allied Powers, accepted the surrender.

Occupation forces bring great changes to Japan. Troops from the United States and the British Commonwealth,* under the command of General MacArthur, occupied Japan after the country surrendered. The occupation forces did not know how they would be greeted by the defeated Japanese. To their surprise, they found most of the people cooperative and even friendly.

The occupation forces remained in Japan for seven years. At first, the leaders of these forces had two main goals—to prevent Japan from ever making war again, and to set up a democratic government in the country. People accused of war crimes were brought to trial and punished.

In 1947 Japan adopted a new constitution. This document gave the people rights and freedoms they had never had before. Reforms were also made in education and the ownership of farmland. (See Chapters 5, 9, and 13.) The new

were bombing Japanese cities. But Japan's leaders still refused to give up.

In the summer of 1945, American leaders had to make a difficult decision. A terrible new weapon, the atomic bomb, had been developed in the United States and was ready to be used. Should this be used against Japan or not? For weeks, scientists and political leaders in the United States argued over this question. Many felt that it was wrong to use a weapon so terrible. Others felt that using the bomb might make Japan surrender sooner, and save the lives of thousands more Americans who would certainly die if a land invasion of Japan was necessary to force surrender. The decision was finally made. In August,

constitution did away with Japan's army and navy. It promised that Japan would never again start a war.

By this time, a worldwide conflict known as the Cold War* had begun. On one side were the Communist nations, such as the Soviet Union. On the other side were democratic nations, such as the United States. The Cold War caused the United States to change its view of Japan. American leaders realized that Japan would be a valuable ally in the Cold War if it were strong and prosperous. Therefore, occupation forces now worked to help the Japanese people rebuild their industries.

Japan gains back its independence. In 1951, Japan signed a peace treaty with the United States and forty-seven other nations. These nations had all been enemies of Japan in World War II. Under the peace treaty, which took effect in 1952, Japan again became an independent country.

Since Japan had no armed forces, the United States took over the task of defending it from possible enemies. Another treaty was signed in 1951. It gave the United States the right to build military bases in Japan and to station troops there.

Cooperation

See page 160

The picture at right shows a group of American and Japanese businessmen at an automobile plant in Japan. Today Japan has friendly relations with the United States and many other countries. Is it important in our modern world for nations to have friendly relations with each other? Is it more important for countries to cooperate with each other today than it was one hundred years ago? Explain your answers.

Japan becomes a prosperous and peace-loving country. After the Occupation ended, the Japanese set to work to make their country more prosperous. They were amazingly successful in reaching this goal. By the middle of the 1960's, Japan had become one of the world's leading industrial nations. (See pages 121-122.)

Meanwhile, the Japanese government worked hard to establish friendly relations with other countries. In 1956, Japan became a full member of the United Nations.* Gradually, most of the problems remaining from World War II were solved. For example, in 1972 the United States returned Oki-

nawa and other islands in the Ryukyu chain to Japan. (See map on page 25.) These islands had been occupied by American troops since 1945. In 1972, Japan also began to have official relations with China for the first time in thirty-five years.

Japan also resumed official relations with another wartime enemy, the Soviet Union. However, a formal peace treaty between the two countries has not yet been signed. Before signing such a treaty, the Japanese would like the Soviets to return four small islands northeast of Hokkaido. Soviet troops have occupied these islands ever since World War II.

Today, Japan holds a position of world leadership. Not only is it one of the most prosperous countries in Asia, but it is also one of the most democratic. It is a strong ally of the United States and other freedom-loving countries. Japan works closely with other nations to encourage the exchange of goods and information. It plays an important role in world organizations such as the United Nations. Japan's government provides both money and experts to help the less developed countries, especially in Asia. Clearly, Japan is making every effort to cooperate with other nations and to keep peace in the world.

5 Government

The people of Japan live in a democracy.
Japan is a free country. A democratic
constitution, which was adopted in
1947, guarantees the rights of every
Japanese citizen. All people in the
country have the right to express their
opinions without fear. They cannot be
held in prison without a court trial, and
they may follow the religion of their
choice. When Japanese men and women
reach the age of twenty, they have the
right to vote for the people who make
their country's laws. All candidates
have an opportunity to say publicly
what they plan to do if they are elected,
and the voters choose their representatives by secret ballot.

**The laws of Japan are made by the
National Diet.** Japan's lawmaking body,
the National Diet, is made up of two
houses. One house, called the House
of Councillors, has 252 members. They
are elected for a period of six years.
The 511 members of the House of
Representatives are elected for four-
year terms.

Japan's constitution guarantees certain basic rights to every citizen. These include the right to express one's opinions without fear. For example, the candidate in the picture at far left is discussing the possibility of revising the constitution. Japanese men and women twenty years of age or older have the right to select their country's lawmakers. (The picture at left shows the posting of election returns.) What are some other rights and freedoms that Japanese citizens enjoy? What are some of the main ways in which government in Japan today differs from government under the Tokugawa shoguns? (See Chapter 3.)

Suggested laws, or bills, become law when passed by both houses of the Diet. In case of disagreement between the two houses, the House of Representatives has an advantage. When a bill fails to pass the House of Councillors, the House of Representatives may vote on the bill again. If two thirds of the members vote for the bill it becomes a law. However, if the House of Representatives rejects a bill, the House of Councillors can do nothing.

The prime minister and the cabinet direct the government. The people who direct Japan's government are the prime minister and the cabinet. The prime minister is chosen by the Diet from among its own members. Usually the leader of the political party that has the most members in the Diet receives this office. The prime minister chooses a group of people to form the cabinet. A majority of these cabinet members must be chosen from among the members of the Diet. They serve as the heads of various departments of the government. Indirectly, then, the people choose their executive leaders.

The prime minister and the cabinet plan many of the important bills that

See page 161

Zenko Suzuki became the prime minister of Japan in 1980. The prime minister and the cabinet direct Japan's government. What are some of their duties? How is the prime minister selected? How are the cabinet members chosen? What might happen to cause the prime minister and the cabinet to resign?

Rules and Government

are introduced in the Diet. They also see that laws made in the Diet are carried out. The prime minister and the cabinet serve as long as they have the support of a majority in the House of Representatives. If they lose this support, they must do one of two things. Either they must resign, or the prime minister must dismiss the House of Representatives and call a national election. The purpose of this election is to choose members of the new House of Representatives. It must be held within forty days.

The emperor is a symbol of the nation. Although Japan is a democracy, it still has an emperor. The emperor serves as a symbol of Japan's long history as an independent nation. Under the constitution of 1947, the emperor does not rule Japan. But he has certain ceremonial duties, such as opening sessions of the Diet and signing new laws. The emperor also appoints the prime minister, who has been chosen by the Diet. Important foreign visitors are received by the emperor when they arrive.

Japan's courts protect the people's rights and freedoms. The Japanese courts explain the laws and decide whether people accused of crimes are guilty or innocent. The courts assure that the rights

Emperor Hirohito opening a session of the Diet, Japan's lawmaking assembly. Hirohito is a descendant of the line of emperors who have occupied the Japanese throne for about fifteen hundred years. Why do you suppose Japan still has an emperor, even though the country now has a democratic form of government? What are the emperor's duties? How do the Japanese people feel about him?

and freedoms of the people, such as the right to a fair trial and freedom of speech, are not violated. The highest court in Japan is the Supreme Court, made up of a chief justice and fourteen associate justices. The Supreme Court decides whether or not laws are in agreement with the constitution, which is the highest law of the land.

Japan also has a number of lower courts under the Supreme Court. Judges in the lower courts are appointed by the cabinet. However, the judges must be chosen from a list of candidates approved by the Supreme Court. Small lawsuits and minor crimes are tried in summary* courts. People who are accused of serious crimes are brought to trial in district courts. If a person feels that the trial has not been fair, the case may be taken to a higher court.

Local government. Japan is divided into forty-seven districts, called prefectures. The people of each prefecture elect a governor and a lawmaking assembly. Each city, town, and village of Japan has an assembly, whose members are also elected by the local citizens.

*See Glossary

A Japanese court. Japan's courts protect the people's rights and freedoms. The highest court, the Supreme Court, decides whether or not laws are in agreement with the constitution.

Thinking Together

Beginning in the 1600's, Japan was closed off from the rest of the world for over 200 years. Discuss the following statement with your classmates. No nation should isolate itself from the rest of the world. You may wish to consider the following questions in your discussion.

1. How did isolation help the Japanese? In what ways was it harmful to them?
2. Could Japan have become the strong industrial nation it is today if it had continued its policy of isolation?
3. Could any major country today successfully follow a policy of isolation?

The suggestions on pages 182 and 183, in the Skills Manual, will help you have a successful discussion.

Be a Biographer

Each of the people listed below played an important part in the history and development of Japan. Select one of the following and write a brief biography.

Emperor Hirohito	Tokugawa Ieyasu
Emperor Meiji	Hideki Tojo
Commodore Perry	Yoritomo

In addition to a brief summary of the person's life, your biography should include information about the ways in which Japan's history was influenced by this person. The suggestions on pages 177-182 will help you to find sources of information and write an interesting biography.

Explore Atomic Energy

In 1945, American leaders made the difficult decision to use a new kind of weapon against the Japanese. In August of that year, atomic bombs were dropped on the cities of Hiroshima and Nagasaki. This action brought the world into the atomic age. Since 1945, scientists have gained much new information about ways of releasing and using energy within the atom. Do research in other sources about atomic energy and prepare an oral report to share with your classmates. This report should include information about the following:

1. the great destructive power of atomic energy
2. peaceful ways in which atomic energy can be used to serve people

The guidelines on pages 177-182 will be helpful to you in preparing your report.

Be a Historian

The Russo-Japanese War, fought in 1904 and 1905, brought Japan recognition as a major world power. Imagine that you are an American historian, and write a magazine article about the Russo-Japanese War. Include information about the following in your article:

1. causes of the war
2. important battles
3. results of the war

To write your article, you will need to do research in outside sources. See pages 177-182, in the Skills Manual, for helpful suggestions.

Make Comparisons

Both Japan and the United States are democracies. However, there are differences between the governments of these two countries. Make a chart for your classroom on which you compare the governments of Japan and the United States. Include information about the following on this chart:

1. rights and freedoms of the people
2. how laws are made
3. chief government officials and their duties
4. how government officials are chosen
5. major political parties
6. local governments

Chapter 5 contains much of the information you will need. You may also wish to do research in other sources.

A Problem To Solve

Although the Japanese people have many ancient traditions, their ways of living have changed greatly over the centuries. How have people in other countries influenced life in Japan? In forming your hypotheses, consider ways in which foreign influences have affected the following:

1. government in Japan
2. religious practices in Japan
3. the Japanese language
4. the arts of Japan
5. ways of earning a living in Japan
6. recreation in Japan
7. life in Japanese cities

The pictures and text in Parts 3 and 4, as well as in Part 2, provide much of the information you will need. You may also wish to do research in other sources.

See Skills Manual, pages 166-169

Part 3
People and Their Way of Life

Although Japan is a small country, it has a very large population. The chapters in Part 3 provide much information about the people of Japan. As you read, try to answer these questions.

- What are the Japanese people like? How does their way of life today differ from ours? In what ways is it similar to ours?
- What are Japan's largest cities? Which of these cities would you especially like to visit?
- What would it be like to live in a typical Japanese village?
- How important is education to the Japanese people? What are Japanese schools like?
- What are some of the ways the Japanese people express their love of beauty?
- How do the Japanese spend their leisure time? What holidays and festivals are important in Japan?

Migration

A busy street in Tokyo. During the present century, large numbers of people in Japan have moved from farms and small villages to towns and cities. Today, about three fourths of Japan's people live in urban areas. What do you suppose are the reasons for the migration* of people from farms to cities? What are some of the advantages of living in a large city such as Tokyo? What problems do people living in large cities face? Some of the chapters in Part 3 and Part 4 provide information that will help you answer these questions.

Snack time for a Japanese family. If you were to visit a Japanese family, you would probably find many similarities between their way of life and yours. What do you suppose some of these likenesses would be? What differences do you think you would find?

6 People

A Crowded Country

Japan is only about the size of the state of California, yet it is the home of about 117 million people. This is a little more than half as many people as live in the United States. Because Japan is a small country with many people, we say it is very densely populated. If all its people were spread evenly throughout the country, there would be about 800 people on each square mile of land. By comparison, the United States has only about 60 people per square mile.

Japan does not face the same problem as other crowded countries in Asia. In these countries, the population is increasing rapidly each year. Although the number of people in Japan grew rapidly after World War II, its rate of population growth now is only about one percent a year.

Where do the Japanese people live? Some parts of Japan are much more crowded than others. Most of Japan's people live on the coastal lowlands in the central and southern parts of the country. The most crowded part of Japan is the area that extends southwestward from Tokyo into northern Kyushu. Some of the best farmland and most of the important industries in Japan are located here. Fewer people live in northern Japan and in the mountainous areas scattered throughout the country.

As a country becomes industrialized, a change usually takes place in its population distribution, or where the people live. People begin to move from farms and villages to towns and cities. This change began to take place in Japan at the end of the nineteenth century and is continuing today. Many of the people who are moving away from the rural areas are young people who want to find better jobs and take part in the more exciting life of the city.

A Problem To Solve

Japan is the home of about 117 million people. This is an average of about 800 people for each square mile of land. As this map shows, however, Japan's population is not distributed evenly. <u>Why are some parts of Japan much more heavily populated than other parts of the country?</u> In forming hypotheses to solve this problem, consider facts about the following:

a. Japan's land features
b. climate in different parts of Japan
c. opportunities for people to earn a living

See Skills Manual, pages 166–169

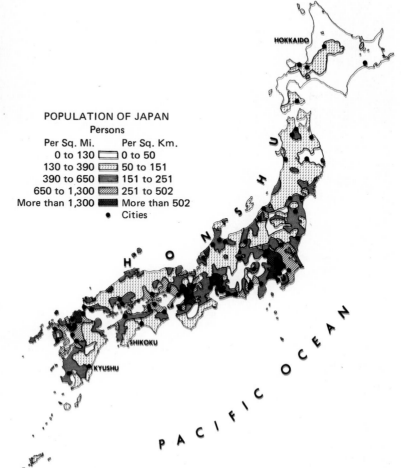

POPULATION OF JAPAN

Persons

Per Sq. Mi.	Per Sq. Km.
0 to 130	0 to 50
130 to 390	50 to 151
390 to 650	151 to 251
650 to 1,300	251 to 502
More than 1,300	More than 502
•	Cities

As this change in population distribution continues, the heavily populated areas of Japan are becoming even more crowded. For example, more than eleven and one-half million people now live in Greater Tokyo. The Japanese government is encouraging industries to move to less crowded parts of the country. It is hoped that in this way people will not have to move to overcrowded areas to find good jobs.

A People With Many Things in Common

The Japanese people look more alike than the people of some other countries. In France and Germany, for instance, some of the people are blond and others have dark hair. Some are short, and others are tall. Nearly all Japanese, however, have straight black hair, tan skin, and dark eyes that appear to be slanted.

Enjoying a Sunday afternoon in Yokohama. The Japanese people share many characteristics in common. For example, almost all Japanese have straight black hair and dark eyes that appear slanted. In general, they are a hardworking and inventive people with a strong national feeling. Do research to discover some reasons why the Japanese are a people with much in common.

They are generally short, although today's young people are somewhat taller than their parents. This is partly because they have better food than their parents had while growing up.

One small group of people in Japan, called the Ainu, differ in appearance from most other Japanese. The Ainu have black, wavy hair and are fair skinned. They are generally short and stocky. Most of the Ainu in Japan live in isolated villages on Hokkaido. At one time they occupied much of Japan. (See page 40.)

What other characteristics do the Japanese people share? People throughout the world differ from each other in personality. Yet, the people of one nation can often be said to share some of the same characteristics of personality. This is especially true of the people of Japan. Generally, the Japanese have a strong national feeling and are proud to be Japanese. They are usually thought of as a very courteous people. Instead of shaking hands to greet each other or to show respect, the Japanese bow slightly from the waist. The modern industrial society built by the Japanese people tells us that they are hardworking and industrious. They are also a very inventive people and have shown great enthusiasm for modern ideas and new ways of life.

How did the Japanese become a people with many things in common? Language has played an important part in making the Japanese a people with many things in common. In some countries, such as India, many different languages and dialects are spoken. When people are unable to communicate with each other, misunderstandings occur. The people sometimes divide into different groups that are hostile to each other. The Japanese, however, have long shared a common language that has helped them feel they belong together.

A study of Japanese history also helps us to understand why they are a people with many things in common. As you read in Chapter 3, the Japanese lived apart from the world for more than two

71

CHANOYU

The Tea Ceremony, or Chanoyu, is a Japanese custom which grew out of tea contests, or parties, once enjoyed by the upper-class people of Japan. Guests at the parties were served tea grown in different parts of the country. Those who could identify the tea raised in the best tea-growing region received prizes. Later, the tea contest was influenced by Zen Buddhism (see page 75), and the purpose of the contest changed. The guests were to enjoy the atmosphere in which the tea was served. Out of tradition, Chanoyu developed into the ceremony it is today.

Chanoyu is a formal ceremony which usually takes place in a small tea house built in a garden. Guests take time to admire the house and the garden. They are also expected to admire the simple decorations within the tea house. As they drink the tea, the guests comment on the beauty of the dishes that are used, and praise the taste of the tea.

A complete Tea Ceremony takes about four hours. First the guests are served a light meal. After the meal they often rest in the garden. Then the main ceremony begins, and the guests are served a thick green tea. Later they are served a lighter, foamy tea.

Chanoyu is more than strict ritual. To the Japanese, Chanoyu is an art and represents a way of living. They feel it is also important that people take time in their everyday lives to find peace within themselves and beauty in simple things.

centuries. During this time, the people were divided into social classes. They were expected to live and act as other people of their class. They were taught to be loyal and to show proper respect and unquestioning obedience to their superiors. This training began in the family. Children were taught loyalty and respect for those in authority, from their fathers to the shogun and the emperor. Even until the end of World War II there were restrictions to keep the people obedient and loyal to their leaders. Children were taught only what the government wanted them to know. Police officers kept a close watch on the activities of the people. These and other controls made certain that the Japanese people thought and acted alike.

The Japanese have a long cultural heritage. Living together in their small island country, the Japanese have developed certain ways of life that have been passed down from parents to children. This long cultural heritage also has helped them to feel that they belong together.

Art of living. For hundreds of years, the Japanese people have been known for their enjoyment of customs that add beauty and graciousness to everyday life. One of these customs is called the Tea Ceremony, or Chanoyu. (See description at left.) This ceremony is meant to help people find beauty in plain and simple things. The Japanese are famous for the art of arranging flowers. They are also famous for their creative, beautiful gardens. (See page 101.) The Japanese feel that activities such as these bring peace of mind—

Arts

This picture shows a young Japanese woman, in traditional costume, arranging a bouquet of flowers in her home. Flower arranging is a Japanese art that adds beauty to everyday life. What are some other arts that are especially enjoyed by the people of Japan? (Chapter 10 provides information that will help you answer this question.) Do you feel it is important for people everywhere to take time in their daily lives to appreciate beauty? Explain your answer.

something that is difficult to achieve in the routine of daily living.

Religion. As in many countries, religion has had an important influence on Japanese culture. The main religions are Shinto and Buddhism, but some Japanese are followers of Christianity.

Shinto is the oldest religion in Japan. It began as a form of nature worship. The early Japanese believed that gods dwelled in the sea, mountains, and throughout the world of nature. Shinto later included the worship of ancestors and heroes. Most of the traditional

See pages 76 - 77

The great bronze statue of Buddha at Kamakura. One way in which the Japanese meet their need for faith is through religion. Buddhism and Shinto are the main religions in Japan today, but Christianity also has Japanese followers. What are some of the ways in which religious beliefs are reflected in the daily lives of people in Japan? Before answering this question, you may wish to do research in other sources as well as in this book. The suggestions on pages 177-179, in the Skills Manual, will be helpful in locating information.

The Need for Faith

festivals and ceremonies held in Japan today are Shinto in origin.

Many Japanese who participate in the ceremonies of Shinto are also Buddhists. Buddhism was brought to Japan from China and Korea in the sixth century. Generally, the followers of Buddhism believe that happiness is to be found by overcoming selfishness and leading a good and kindly life. They also place emphasis on the unimportance of the material things of life.

There are several main forms of Buddhism in Japan. One of these is Zen Buddhism. Followers of this form of Buddhism spend much time in strict meditation. Zen Buddhism has had an important influence on the arts of Japan, such as the Tea Ceremony. Since World War II, another Buddhist group, called Soka Gakkai, has gained political strength in Japan. Members of Soka Gakkai feel strongly that theirs is the only true religion. In political elections it is a duty for them to vote for the candidates approved by their religious organization.

Christianity was first brought to Japan in 1549. However, for many years the Christian religion was banned in Japan. (See page 45.) During the reign of Emperor Meiji* this ban was lifted, and Christianity began to grow. Even so, there are still only about 870,000 Japanese Christians.

<u>Family life</u>. Family life is an important part of the heritage of the Japanese people. For hundreds of years the Japanese followed strict family customs. Japanese children were taught to treat their parents, ancestors, and anyone in authority with great respect. They were also taught that poor behavior of any sort would disgrace the family. When children were old enough to marry, their parents chose their marriage partners. Very often the bride and groom were almost strangers. The oldest son of the Japanese family did not become independent of his family even after marriage. Instead, he brought his new wife into the family household. When the father grew old or died, the oldest son became head of the household. Many of these customs changed after World War II, giving Japanese youths much more freedom.

*See Glossary

75

Needs

The people of Japan, like all other people on the earth, must meet certain basic needs in order to be healthy and happy. Scientists who study human behavior tell us that these basic needs are almost exactly the same for all people, whatever their skin color, national origin, or religion may be. Whether people are rich or poor, they have the same basic needs.

There are three kinds of basic needs. They are: physical needs, social needs, and the need for faith.

Physical Needs

Some basic needs are so important that people will die or become very ill if they fail to meet them. These are physical needs. They include the need for:

1. air
2. water
3. food
4. protection from heat and cold
5. sleep and rest
6. exercise

Although all people share these needs, they do not all meet them in the same way. How do you meet your physical needs? How do you think people in Japan meet their physical needs?

Social Needs

People also have social needs. Each person must meet these needs in order to have a happy and useful life. Social needs include:

1. Belonging to a group. All people need to feel they belong to a group of people who respect them and whom they respect. Belonging to a family is one of the main ways people meet this need. What can the members of a family do to show that they love and respect each other? How do the members of your family help one another? Do you think family life is important to the people of Japan? Why do you think this?

Having friends also helps people meet their need for belonging to a group. What groups of friends do you have? Why are these people your friends? Do you suppose young people in Japan enjoy doing the same kinds of things with their friends as you enjoy doing with your friends? Why? Why not?

2. Goals. To be happy, every person needs goals to work for. What goals do you want to reach? How can working toward these goals help you have a happy life? What kinds of goals do you think young people in Japan have?

3. A chance to think and learn. All people need a chance to develop and use their abilities. They need opportunities to find out about things that make them curious. What would you like to learn? How can you learn these things? How can developing your abilities help you have a happy life? Is it important for people in Japan to have a chance to think and learn? to make decisions for themselves? Why? Why not?

4. A feeling of accomplishment. You share with every other person the need for a feeling of accomplishment. All people need to feel that their lives are successful in some way. What gives you a feeling of accomplishment? Can you imagine what life would be like if you never had this feeling?

The Need for Faith

In addition to physical and social needs, all people also have a need for faith. You need to believe that life is precious and that the future is something to look for-

Playing ball at a park in Yokohama. Which basic needs are these young people meeting? Explain.

ward to. You may have different kinds of faith, including:

1. Faith in yourself. In order to feel secure, you must have faith in your own abilities. You must feel that you will be able to do some useful work in the world and that you will be generally happy. You must believe that you can work toward solving whatever problems life brings to you. How do you think you can build faith in yourself?

2. Faith in other people. You also need to feel that you can count on other people to do their part and to help you when you need help. What people do you have faith in? What do you think life would be like without this kind of faith?

3. Faith in nature's laws. Another kind of faith that helps people face the future with confidence is faith in nature's laws. The more we learn about our universe, the more certain we feel that we can depend on nature. How would you feel if you couldn't have faith in nature's laws?

4. Religious faith. Throughout history, almost all people have had some kind of religious faith. Religion can help people understand themselves and the world they live in. It can bring them joy, and it can give them confidence in times of trouble. Religion can also help people live together happily. For example, most religions teach people to be honest and to love and help their neighbors. In what ways do people in Japan express their religious faith?

Most People in Japan Are Able To Meet Their Basic Needs

Most people in Japan have an opportunity to meet the three kinds of basic needs we have explored here. Some do not, however. For example, many city families cannot find adequate housing.

Why do you think so many Japanese have a good way of life? What is the government doing to help those people who are unable to meet their needs? Do research in this book and in other sources to find information that will help you answer these questions.

Loyalty

See page 164

A Japanese family enjoying a Sunday walk. For centuries, Japanese young people were expected to obey their parents and other older relatives without question. For example, they usually had to accept the husbands or wives their parents chose for them. In recent years, however, the idea of unquestioning loyalty to one's family has been challenged. Why do you suppose this is so? Do you think this change in Japanese family life is good or bad? Do you believe that some loyalty is important to family life? Give reasons for your answers. (You may wish to discuss these questions with your classmates.)

A Changing Nation

Vast changes have come to Japan in the last forty years. First there was the shock of Japan's defeat in World War II. (See page 57.) This caused many Japanese to question traditional ideas and ways of living. During the years that followed, a democratic government was set up in Japan for the first time. Important changes were also made in farming and education. As time passed, Japan recovered from the war and began to develop new industries. Many Japanese farmers left their native villages and moved to the cities. There they took jobs in factories and offices. As a result, the cities grew larger than ever before. Today Japan is a modern industrial nation with a high standard of living.

Old ways of thinking and living are being challenged. When great changes take place in a country, people begin to live differently from the way they did before. They also form new attitudes toward life. This has been happening in Japan. For example, people are no longer expected to obey their leaders without question. Family life in Japan is becoming more like our own. Also, Japanese women have more freedom

78

than they used to. Many women now have careers outside the home.

The Japanese are adjusting to all these changes with amazing speed. However, strong traditions are not easy for any people to change. Some of the older Japanese, especially, miss the rules and customs that once guided their lives. Will the total effect of these changes on the Japanese people be good or bad? Only time will tell.

The old and the new. The Japanese have found a way to overcome many of the uncertainties of change. They simply combine new ways of life with the old. For instance, new buildings in Japan have a modern look. Yet they also show the influence of traditional Japanese architecture. The lives of many Japanese also show a blending of old and new. In the cities, people may ride home from their modern offices on a subway. When they arrive home, they are likely to change their Western-style clothing for comfortable kimonos.* They may sit on soft mats and eat dinner at a low table. Probably they will be just as courteous as their parents and grandparents before them. In these and other ways, the Japanese blend the modern and traditional ways of life.

7 Cities

A country of many cities. As you make plans to visit some of Japan's largest and most interesting cities, you glance at your map. You find it hard to imagine that a hundred years ago the only large cities in this country were Tokyo, Kyoto, and Osaka. For centuries, most of the people in Japan were farmers or craft workers who lived in small towns and villages. Then, in the last half of the nineteenth century, the Japanese learned to use modern machinery and

modern manufacturing methods. Factories were built in towns and villages. As more people came to work in the factories, many of these towns and villages grew into cities. Today, about three fourths of Japan's people live in or near towns and cities. As you study your map, you decide that you will begin your visit in Tokyo.

Tokyo, the capital of Japan. You are now flying across Tokyo Bay toward one of the largest cities in the world. This is Tokyo, which has a population of more than 8,600,000. Tokyo is by far the most important city in Japan—the political capital as well as the leading industrial and cultural center of the country.

Tokyo and the towns and cities near it have grown so close together that you cannot tell where one city ends and another begins. They form one huge urban area. About 11,623,000 people live in this urban area, which is known as Greater Tokyo. (See map on page 87.)

You are approaching Tokyo's airport now. Below you is the crowded waterfront of Tokyo Bay. Ahead you see factory chimneys and the tops of tall buildings. Beyond these, a blanket of housetops spreads out across the countryside. Many canals branch off the Sumida River, which winds through part of Tokyo. Expressways lead like long, concrete ribbons to the heart of the city.

After landing at the airport, you get into a taxicab to ride downtown.

A Problem To Solve
The picture at left shows traffic in downtown Tokyo, one of the largest cities in the world. How did Tokyo become such a great city? In forming hypotheses to solve this problem, you will need to consider facts about the following:
1. Tokyo's location
2. its history
3. transportation facilities
4. the influence of important ideas and ways of living (see pages 160-164)

See Skills Manual, pages 166 – 169

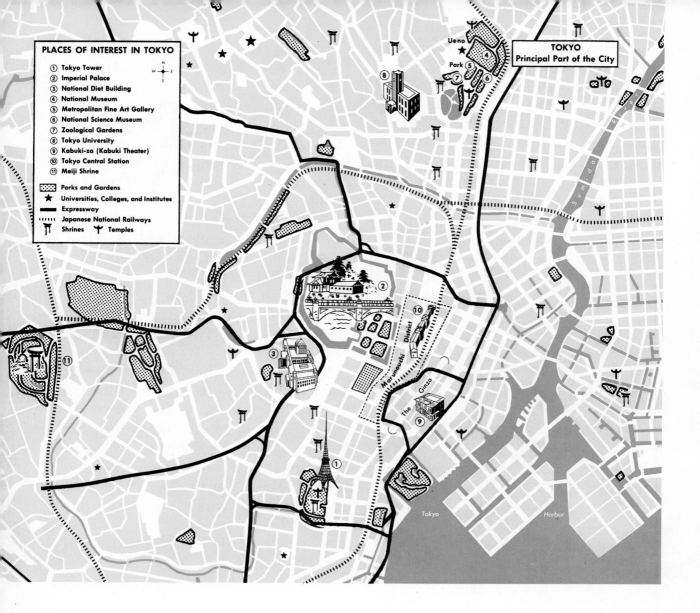

PLACES OF INTEREST IN TOKYO

① Tokyo Tower
② Imperial Palace
③ National Diet Building
④ National Museum
⑤ Metropolitan Fine Art Gallery
⑥ National Science Museum
⑦ Zoological Gardens
⑧ Tokyo University
⑨ Kabuki-za (Kabuki Theater)
⑩ Tokyo Central Station
⑪ Meiji Shrine

▨ Parks and Gardens
★ Universities, Colleges, and Institutes
━ Expressway
⋯ Japanese National Railways
卂 Shrines   丫 Temples

TOKYO
Principal Part of the City

When you reach your hotel, you find that it is a large, modern building with beautifully decorated rooms. Looking out of your hotel windows, you see some of the other new buildings in downtown Tokyo. They are constructed of concrete, steel, aluminum, and glass.

Through your hotel windows, you also notice that traffic is very heavy. It is rush hour, and automobiles, buses, trucks, and motorcycles move slowly forward, bumper to bumper. Tokyo, with its huge population, has serious traffic problems. Sometimes it takes half an hour to go one downtown block.

The Imperial Palace. It is a fairly short walk from your hotel to a section of Tokyo called the Imperial Palace. This area includes the modern palace where the emperor of Japan now makes his home, as well as parts of the old palace where Japan's emperors lived for many years. Most of the Imperial Palace is open to visitors only on New Year's Day and on the emperor's birthday. However, you can visit the beautiful

A section of Tokyo called the Imperial Palace. The emperor of Japan makes his home here.

grounds of the East Imperial Garden, which is open to the public the year around. The East Imperial Garden contains the ruins of an ancient castle and its moat. A high stone wall rises along the moat, and a line of gnarled old pine trees borders the wall. You may also want to stroll through the Imperial Palace Plaza. This is a public park and playground in front of the main entrance to the Imperial Palace.

Tokyo from past to present. Tokyo has not always been the capital of Japan. In early times, it was just a small village called Edo. The Japanese emperor and his court lived in the city of Kyoto. Then, in the seventeenth century, the first Tokugawa shogun made Edo his capital. (See page 44.) During the period of Tokugawa rule, Edo became a great city. In 1868, its name was changed to Tokyo, and it became the headquarters of the Meiji emperor's government.

Twice during the twentieth century, Tokyo has suffered great destruction. In 1923, a violent earthquake struck the city. The earthquake destroyed many buildings, but the spreading fires did most of the damage. Within a few hours, most of the city lay in ruins and 59,000 people were dead. The Japanese quickly rebuilt Tokyo, but in World War II, it was again almost destroyed. Many buildings were bombed, and more than half of the people were killed or forced to leave the city.

Today it is hard to realize that Tokyo ever suffered serious destruction. Almost no signs of war damage remain. Tokyo is now a city of tall buildings and modern freeways, sprawling factories and busy shopping centers.

Several places of interest in Tokyo. Walking a few blocks southwest of the Imperial Palace, you see the National Diet Building, where the laws of Japan are made. South of the Diet building you see a tall structure. This is Tokyo Tower, a 1,092-foot-high radio and television spire.

You can spend several days visiting the many beautiful parks in Tokyo. Important public buildings are located in some of them. In Ueno Park, the largest in the city, you can visit the National Museum, the Metropolitan Fine Art Gallery, and the National Science Museum. (See map on page 82.) This park also has one of the largest zoos in Japan. When the cherry trees blossom in early April, Ueno Park is especially beautiful.

One evening you walk through Tokyo's main shopping district, called the Ginza. This district, with its brilliant neon lights, extends for about half a mile through the busiest part of the city. The department stores, restaurants, tearooms, and sidewalk shops here are brightly lighted, and the streets are crowded with people.

Problems of a growing city. Tokyo faces serious problems because of its swift growth. You have already noticed the problem of heavy traffic in this city. Also, there is not enough good housing for all of Tokyo's people. In much of the city, the houses are small and flimsy. Many homes in Greater Tokyo are not served by a sewage system.

Pollution of air and water is another serious problem in Tokyo. Factories and motor vehicles give off large amounts of harmful fumes. As a result, the air is often dark and smoky and has an unpleasant smell. Waste materials from homes and factories have polluted Tokyo Bay and the streams that flow into it.

Today, efforts are being made to solve Tokyo's problems. To provide better housing, the city government is helping to build many modern apartment buildings in Tokyo. New expressways and subway lines are also being built. These should make it easier to travel from one part of Tokyo to another. Laws have been passed to reduce air and water pollution. For example, cars must now be equipped with devices that keep harmful fumes from going into the air. Also, new cities and towns are growing up in rural areas outside of Tokyo. These may help to relieve overcrowding in the central part of the city.

Yokohama. The city of Yokohama is only about twenty miles from downtown Tokyo. It is part of the great urban area that extends along the west-

Yokohama is Japan's third largest city and one of its leading ports. It has some of the same problems that large cities in our country face. What do you suppose these problems are?

ern shore of Tokyo Bay. (See map on page 87.) As you travel by train from Tokyo to Yokohama, you feel as though you are going from one part to another part of a single huge city.

Yokohama is Japan's third largest city with a population of more than 2,600,000. Before Japan was opened to foreign trade, Yokohama was just a fishing village. In 1859, Yokohama's port was opened to foreign traders and it began to grow rapidly. Today, Yokohama is one of the most important port cities in Japan.

After lunch, you walk to the waterfront. You see some workers building and repairing ships in one of the modern shipyards. Other workers are loading huge freighters with goods such as automobiles, electrical equipment, and

textiles. These are some of the main products that are exported to foreign countries from Yokohama.

Nagoya. From Yokohama, you take the train to the city of Nagoya, at the head of Ise Bay. (See map on page 25.) It lies between Tokyo, the present-day capital of Japan, and Kyoto, an ancient capital of the country. Because of its location, Nagoya is sometimes called the "Middle Capital."

Soon after you arrive, you visit Nagoya Castle. This great fortress was built by a Japanese warrior in 1612. It was destroyed during World War II, but has since been rebuilt. Nagoya Castle was only one of several fortresses that were constructed long ago in this area. The city of Nagoya began as a small village surrounding these ancient fortifications. Today, it is the fourth largest city in Japan and the home of more than 2,000,000 people.

Nagoya is an industrial city of major importance in Japan. People who work in its factories make such goods as automobiles, bicycles, and woolen textiles. Much of Japan's chinaware and pottery is produced in Nagoya.

Kyoto. From Nagoya, you travel to the inland city of Kyoto. High, green hills border the plain on which this city lies. A few miles to the northeast is beautiful Lake Biwa. (See map on page 25.) For more than one thousand years, Kyoto was the capital of Japan. Today, about 1,460,000 people live here, and it is the fifth largest city in the country.

Kyoto looks almost like a storybook city. As you drive through the streets, you pass many beautiful temples. You visit ancient palaces and walk through some of the most beautiful gardens in Japan. In small home workshops you watch skilled craft workers weaving silk and embroidering delicate designs on lovely fabrics. In the shop windows you see lacquer* ware and other beautiful articles made by the craft workers of this city. More than any other city in the country, Kyoto has kept the charm and atmosphere of old Japan.

Osaka. A short trip southward takes you from Kyoto to Osaka. This bustling city is located at the mouth of the Yodo River on beautiful Osaka Bay.

*See Glossary

A **public square** in Nagoya, one of Japan's largest and most important industrial cities. What evidence do you see in the picture that Nagoya is a modern city?

(See map on this page.) Soon after you enter Osaka, you drive down the wide Midosuji Boulevard. Large department stores and modern office buildings line this busy thoroughfare. Now your car crosses a bridge over one of the many canals that wind through the city.

Later, you climb a hill to Osaka Castle. From the castle you look out across the city. Housetops and factory chimneys stretch out before you in all directions. About 2,780,000 people live in Osaka. It is the second largest city in Japan. The textile factories, steel mills, and chemical plants located here have helped to make Osaka one of the country's most important industrial and trading cities.

CITIES

- ■ 300,000 to 500,000
- ◻ 500,000 to 1,000,000
- ○ 1,000,000 and Over
- ◉ Greater Tokyo 11,623,000
- ◦ Other Places in Text

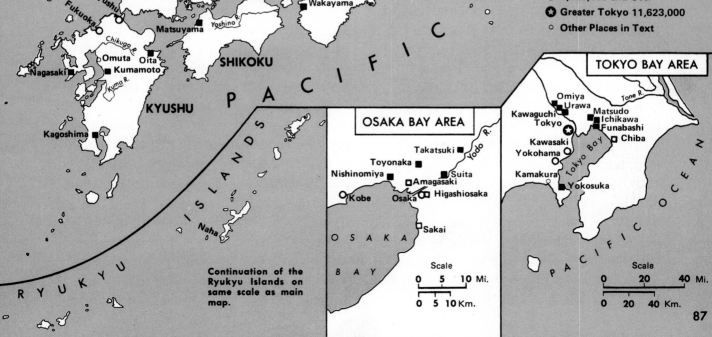

TOKYO BAY AREA

OSAKA BAY AREA

Continuation of the Ryukyu Islands on same scale as main map.

Scale
0   5   10 Mi.
0   5   10 Km.

Scale
0   20   40 Mi.
0   20   40 Km.

Kobe, located along the shores of Osaka Bay, is one of Japan's leading ports. This city's mild and pleasant climate attracts many tourists. Why does Kobe have a mild climate?

As you look to the west, you can see Osaka Bay. Some of the ships anchored at the docks are unloading cargoes of raw materials from foreign countries. The freighters just leaving the bay are carrying manufactured goods produced in the factories of this area. Osaka's fine location has made it such an important trade center that it has been called the "City of Merchants." In 1970, Osaka hosted the first official world's fair ever held in Asia.

Kobe. From Osaka you go to Kobe, another important city on Osaka Bay. Kobe began as a small fishing village and has grown to be the sixth largest city in Japan, with a population of about 1,360,000. It is also one of the country's leading ports. When you walk along the waterfront, you notice that the harbor is divided into two sections. Japanese ships come to one section and

foreign ships to the other. A passerby tells you that many European vessels make Kobe their first stop in Japan.

From the waterfront you look up toward the homes built on the slopes of the Rokko Mountains, which border the city on the north. These mountains are part of a range which shelters Kobe from cold winter winds. They help the city to have a mild, pleasant climate that attracts many tourists. During your stay, you visit some of the beautiful hotels and golf courses in this area. Also, you sunbathe on one of the white, sandy beaches near the city.

Kitakyushu. The next city you visit is Kitakyushu, on the northern coast of the island of Kyushu. This city was formed in 1963 when five smaller cities joined together. It has a population of more than 1,060,000. To reach Kitakyushu by train, you travel through a tunnel beneath a narrow strip of water called the Kammon Strait. This strait separates the islands of Honshu and Kyushu. If you had wished, you could have driven an automobile from Honshu to Kyushu through a highway tunnel or over a new highway bridge.

Much of your time in Kitakyushu is spent visiting factories, for this is one of the important manufacturing cities in Japan. This area has become important in manufacturing partly because it is located near the Kyushu coalfields. Also, there are good ports in the Kitakyushu area, to which ships bring raw materials needed by industry.

Sapporo. Before you leave Japan, you fly to Sapporo, on the island of Hokkaido. From the air, you see the city spread out below, almost surrounded by a wilderness of forested mountains and sparkling blue lakes.

Sapporo is Hokkaido's largest city and most important industrial center. More than 1,240,000 people live here. During your visit, you see textile mills, food-processing plants, and other factories. Sapporo is also the home of a university and several colleges.

You notice that Sapporo looks more like an American city than a traditional Japanese city. This is because Sapporo was laid out by American engineers more than one hundred years ago. It is easy to find your way around Sapporo, with its wide, straight streets arranged in a checkerboard pattern.

Sapporo has excellent winter weather for sports such as skiing and skating. The Winter Olympics were held here in 1972. Today there are a number of fine ski slopes and an enormous skating rink in the Sapporo area. The city has many modern hotels and restaurants to serve visitors.

Sapporo during its annual snow festival. Nearly one fifth of Hokkaido's people live in Sapporo, which is by far the island's largest city.

89

The shopkeepers' section of a Japanese village. Although about three fourths of Japan's people live in or near towns and cities, there are still many rural communities in Japan.

8 Village Life

You are on a bus traveling slowly over a winding, bumpy road to a little village in central Kyushu. You ride through forested mountains and across stretches of flat farmland. Now the road follows a rushing river to a small, flat plain surrounded by mountains. Ahead, you see several clusters of low, thatch-roofed or tile-roofed houses in the midst of rice fields. A few more clusters of houses cling to the slopes of the mountains nearby.

This village looks different from the villages you are accustomed to seeing.

In the United States, a village has only one cluster of houses and shops, built close together. Here, however, you can count twelve small clusters of houses, widely separated by fields and forests. These clusters are called *buraku*. Each one is a little community in itself. Most of the *buraku* are built on the plain. The people who live here are mainly rice farmers. Villagers in the nearby mountain *buraku* raise mushrooms, bees, and tea, or work in the forest.

In the *buraku* you are entering now, small wooden shops stand on either

90

A village school. Many villages in Japan are up-to-date communities with their own schools and modern conveniences such as electricity.

side of the road. This is the shopkeepers' section of the village. People from the forest and farming *buraku* come here to buy the things they need. On your right is the general store. Here the villagers buy food, dishes, clothing, and many other articles. Across the road is the village mill. You get off the bus in front of the store of the tofu-maker.* Farther down the street you see the barbershop, the bicycle repair shop, and the police station.

When you turn off the main road of the shopkeepers' *buraku*, you pass the village office. People from all of the

buraku come here each year to pay their taxes. The clerk at this office records all births, deaths, and marriages in the village. The village assembly also meets here to discuss the affairs of the community. A few minutes' walk from the village office, you come to the post office and the office of the farmers' cooperative.* Farmers from the different *buraku* bring their rice and wheat to the cooperative to be sold. They also buy fertilizer and tools here.

After you leave the shopkeepers' section, you visit the newest *buraku* of the village. The neat, trim houses here

*See Glossary

91

are made of sturdy cement blocks, and they have tiled roofs.

Now you follow a narrow dirt path to one of the older *buraku*. The houses here have heavy, thatched roofs hanging low over their outer walls. Some of these walls are sliding wooden panels. They have been pushed aside to allow fresh air and sunlight to enter the rooms. All the houses seem quiet and empty, for nearly everyone is working in the rice fields.

Mr. and Mrs. Hoshino have invited you to visit their home. As you walk across the yard that surrounds the house, you see fruit trees, a flower bed, and a bamboo pole on which clothes are drying. Among the small sheds in

The kitchen of a village home. Some of the newer houses in Japanese villages are built of cement blocks and have tiled roofs. The homes of the more prosperous families have modern kitchens with electric stoves and other appliances. Older houses usually have wooden walls and thatched roofs. In many of these homes, the kitchen has a charcoal stove that is used for cooking.

the yard are a storehouse for rice, and a bathhouse.

Now you take off your shoes and step onto the narrow porch, which extends most of the way around the house. Shoes would soil the soft, straw mats that cover the floors of the rooms.

Because you are a special guest, Mrs. Hoshino invites you into the parlor. This room is very neat and clean, with a view of the garden outside. You sit down on a cushion, and your hostess places a tray in front of you. On the tray are some cookies and soybean cakes. Mrs. Hoshino bows very low, and fills a cup for you from a small teapot.

When you have finished your tea, your hostess invites you to have supper with the family at the dining table in the kitchen. On the table are chopsticks and several bowls and plates. On the plates are slices of raw fish, boiled fish, vegetables, and pickles. Some of the bowls contain soup, and others are filled with rice. You finish the meal with more tea.

After supper you join the Hoshino children in the family room and enjoy a good television program. Near the center of this room is a square fire pit. The members of the family spend much of their leisure time around the cozy fire. In winter, meals are usually served in this room. Although there is an electric stove in the kitchen, some foods are cooked right here over the fire.

Sliding paper screens separate the family room from the rest of the house. Later, as there are no bedrooms in the house, you go back to the parlor to sleep. Mrs. Hoshino brings you some large quilts. She piles some of them on the floor for a mattress. Then she gives you a small pillow and a light blanket.

Before breakfast the Hoshino family worships together. First they bow before an altar that contains a small image of Buddha* and two wooden tablets on which the names of Mr. Hoshino's ancestors are written. Then they worship at a small altar that was built in honor of Shinto gods.

After a breakfast of rice, *miso** soup, and tea, you thank your hosts and say farewell. Then you return to the shopkeepers' *buraku* to catch your bus. The Hoshinos go to the rice fields for another day of work.

In a Japanese classroom. The Japanese are among the world's best-educated people. In what ways is a Japanese elementary school similar to an elementary school in our country? How is it different?

9 Education

Education has long been important in Japan. Ever since early times, the Japanese people have had a great respect for education. Under the Tokugawa rulers, the Japanese made great advances in art and literature, and in their way of living. (See pages 44-45.) Since it was a time of peace, warriors were encouraged to spend much of their time in study. The Tokugawa leaders provided schools for the children of warriors. Common people could send their children to temple schools run by Buddhist priests.

After the Meiji emperor came to power in the late 1860's, even more importance was placed on education. Japanese leaders wanted their country to become a modern industrial nation like the United States. To reach this goal, Japan needed a large number of well-educated people.

In 1872 the Japanese government started a system of public education. All children were required to attend school for six years. As time passed, many new schools and universities were started throughout Japan.

Before the war, Japanese students were taught only those things the government wanted them to believe. For example, they were taught to obey without question the orders of people in authority. After the war, students were given more freedom. They were taught to think for themselves. In this way, they would be better prepared to carry out their duties as citizens of a democracy.

Japan is a nation of well-educated people. Today the Japanese are among the best-educated people in the world. Almost one hundred percent of the people are able to read and write. Most of the young people attend high school, and many go on to universities. Japan has a large supply of well-educated business people, teachers, scientists, and artists. Highly trained people such as these have made it possible for Japan to become a world leader.

A day in a Japanese elementary school. The morning sun shines down on a three-storied, white schoolhouse. It sparkles on the large windows that extend across the front of the building. Laughing children are walking across the big playground toward the front steps. It is almost eight o'clock, and classes are about to begin.

We follow some of the students into the school and down a corridor to the sixth-grade room. There are thirty-eight children in this classroom. They stand behind their desks until the teacher enters the room. Then the teacher and the students bow politely to each other and take their seats. After roll call, the students leave their room and join the other classes in the gymnasium. Here they see a movie about health.

After World War II, some important changes took place in Japan's system of education. Formerly, boys and girls had been required to attend separate public schools after elementary school. Now, however, they were allowed to go to public school together. Also, Japanese students were required to attend school for nine years instead of six. After the war, the national government no longer controlled education as completely as it had done before. Instead, a board of education was appointed in each city and village of Japan. These boards took over many of the duties of running the schools.

When the students return to their classroom they prepare for language class. On their desks they place fine-tipped brushes, paper, and small, black sticks of dried ink. They rub these sticks in little containers of water to make ink. Then they begin to copy their lesson. With careful brushstrokes, they paint picturelike symbols. Each of these stands for a separate word or idea. One girl tells us that the symbol she is painting stands for "flower." This writing, called calligraphy, is also a form of art. The lines are not merely script with a fixed form but are a means of expressing beauty.

Later in the morning, the students study reading, arithmetic, social studies, and science. They do not use ink and brushes during these classes. Instead, they use pencils and pens.

After lunch it is time to go out of doors for physical education classes. After exercising, the students play a game of dodge ball. When their afternoon studies begin, they are given another lesson in the Japanese language. This time students practice reading

Language

See page 162

Schoolchildren writing picture symbols. The Japanese generally use picture symbols to write their language. (See opposite page.) However, schoolchildren in Japan also learn to read and write with the letters of the Roman alphabet. Do you think it would have been more difficult for you to learn to read and write if English were written in picture symbols? Explain your answer. Why do you suppose the Japanese continue to use this system instead of changing entirely to the use of the Roman alphabet?

The spoken language. There are several different forms of the Japanese language. Three of these forms, or styles, are referred to as the plain, the polite, and the honorific. The speaker chooses the style that will be used according to his or her social standing, the social standing of the person being spoken to, and the subject being discussed. At home, for example, a Japanese person would use the plain style.

The written language. In the fourth century A.D., the Japanese people borrowed the Chinese system of writing. They began to use Chinese picture words, called *kanji*, to write their own Japanese language.

Today the Japanese still use *kanji*, but they also use symbols called *kana*. *Kana* stand for different sounds and are put together to make words. Both *kana* and *kanji* are usually written in columns from the top of a page to the bottom. The Japanese read the columns beginning with the one on the right of the page and moving to the left.

The Japanese language is considered very difficult. For example, just to read the daily newspapers in Japan, a person needs to remember about 1,800 *kanji*. In addition to learning to read and write both *kana* and *kanji* symbols, Japanese schoolchildren also learn to read and write with the letters of the Roman alphabet. The chart below shows the different ways in which Japanese words may be written. The symbols may be drawn with a brush in the way pictured on the opposite page, or they may be written with a pen or pencil.

Symbols that stand for whole words. Each of the four picture symbols shown below is a *kanji*, which stands for an entire Japanese word. After World War II, the Japanese government simplified the language by reducing the number of *kanji* for general use. Many *kanji* shapes were also made simpler.

人 person　花 flower

口 mouth　箸 chopstick

Symbols that stand for sounds. Each of the symbols shown below is a *kana*, which stands for a sound in much the same way that a Roman letter or a group of letters stands for a particular sound. The Japanese use two groups of *kana*. There are about fifty *kana* in each group. One group is called *katakana* and the other is called *hiragana*.

For each sound the Japanese use, there is a *hiragana* symbol and a *katakana* symbol. *Hiragana* symbols are used in everyday writing, as in letters, books, and newspapers. The Japanese mainly use *katakana* symbols much as we use italics in English. Here are a few of the *kana* the Japanese people use, and their corresponding sounds in Roman letters.

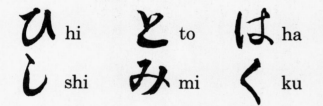

ひ hi　と to　は ha
し shi　み mi　く ku

き ki　も mo　の no
ち chi　な na　あ a

The Japanese use these sound symbols called *kana* in forming words, just as letters are used to form words. You can see how these *kana* are put together to form the following words.

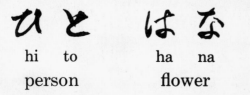

ひ と　　は な
hi to　　ha na
person　　flower

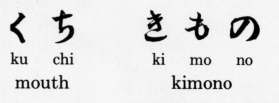

く ち　　き も の
ku chi　　ki mo no
mouth　　kimono

Roman letters. The Japanese write their language with the letters of the Roman alphabet as well as with *kanji* and *kana* symbols. Roman letters or groups of Roman letters represent the same sounds as Japanese *kana* symbols. These letter symbols are put together to form words such as the following.

hi　to　　ha　na
hito　　hana
person　　flower

ku　chi　　ki　mo　no
kuchi　　kimono
mouth　　kimono

and writing with the letters of the Roman alphabet. Later they have classes in art and handicrafts. On some days students have music class at this time. At three o'clock they are dismissed from school.

In Japan, children begin elementary school when they are six years old. However, many have already gone to kindergarten for a year or more before they enter regular school. Elementary school in Japan includes grades one through six.

The Japanese school year does not begin in September, as ours does. Instead, it begins on the first of April.

High school students in art class. Japanese students study art, music, and foreign languages in addition to basic subjects such as science and mathematics.

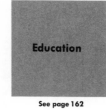

Education

See page 162

A Problem To Solve

The government of Japan believes it is very important for the Japanese people to be well educated. Why is this so?

In solving this problem, consider facts about the following: (1) Japan's form of government; (2) ways of earning a living in Japan; and (3) Japan's position in the world today. Other chapters provide additional information that will help you solve this problem.

See Skills Manual, pages 166-169

The year is divided into three terms, which last from April to July, September to December, and January to March. Between the terms are vacation periods. During summer vacation students may be given homework assignments such as keeping a diary of the weather or collecting butterflies, shells, or flowers.

High schools in Japan. After Japanese students complete elementary school, they enter junior high school. This school includes the seventh through the ninth grades. Students in junior high school continue their study of language, science, mathematics, and social studies. They have courses in music and art. Most students learn to read and write a little of the English language during these years. They may also take special courses in workshop, agriculture, or homemaking.

When girls and boys in Japan reach the age of fifteen, they are no longer required to go to school. However, about 85 percent of the students who finish junior high school continue their education in high school. Japanese high schools are very crowded. In order to be admitted, students must pass entrance examinations.

All high school students in Japan are required to take certain courses. These include courses in the Japanese language, social studies, mathematics, science, a foreign language, health, and physical education. Students who plan to go on to college after finishing high school take advanced courses in most of these subjects. Students who do not plan to go on to college can choose courses that will train them for careers in such fields as manufacturing, business, farming, and nursing.

Colleges and universities in Japan. Almost two million students attend Japanese colleges and universities. These students specialize in fields such as law, medicine, education, engineering, or literature.

There are more than four hundred universities in Japan. Among the largest of these is Tokyo University. In addition there are about five hundred junior colleges and sixty technical colleges.

A Japanese garden is as much a work of art as a painting or a poem. It is designed to create a perfect universe in miniature and to provide a peaceful place in which to think.

10 Arts and Crafts

Perhaps in no other country of the world is so much beauty expressed in everyday life as in Japan. Beauty is found not only in museums, art galleries, and theaters, but also in gardens and homes of the Japanese people. Patiently, Japanese artists and craft workers create paintings, porcelain vases, lacquer* ware, and textiles of exquisite loveliness. Let's explore some of the many ways in which the Japanese people express their love of beauty.

*See Glossary

Arts

Art in gardens and homes. It is twilight in a Japanese garden. You and I sit upon two rocks beside a quiet pool. The air is fragrant with the scent of wisteria and pine. Red azaleas near the garden walls look pink and shadowy in the fading light. Around us are a few green shrubs, moss-covered rocks, and two gnarled, old trees. A small, stone lantern stands in the cool darkness of one corner. There is no sound but the hum of insects and the song of a bird sitting on a branch of a plum tree.

This garden is as much a work of art as a painting, poem, or song. It is a make-believe world made from the beauties of nature. Rocks are used to represent mountains, a little pool for the sea, and two trees for a forest.

Close to the shrubs and rocks at one side of the garden is a low, rambling house. The house seems to be a part of the natural beauty around it. Most of the walls are really sliding doors. When these are open, the garden can be seen from almost every room. The framework of the house is made of unpainted wood, and the roof is blue-gray tile. How well these colors blend with the trees, earth, and sky!

Many homes and gardens in Japan are made in this way. Temples, palaces, and the homes of wealthy people are usually larger and more elaborate. Their gardens may contain graceful bridges, great boulders, small lakes, streams, and woods. In some there are only a few rocks and wide stretches of sandy ground. However, the quiet, natural beauty you find here is found in all of them.

Flower arrangement. There is a special place in the main room of this Japanese home for objects of great beauty. This is an alcove called the tokonoma. On the back wall of the tokonoma hangs a long picture-scroll. Below is a tall, slender vase, which holds a lovely arrangement of flowers.

In Japan, flower arrangement is an art. It is one of the ways in which the people express their love for the beauty of nature. Many of the Japanese learn the art of arranging flowers from special teachers. However, you do not see large, colorful bouquets in all rooms of the house. Instead, there is only one simple flower arrangement in the tokonoma. The Japanese are taught to make a few blossoms and twigs look as though they are really growing. (See picture on page 73.)

Painting. Many Japanese paintings express the same love for nature that is shown in the gardens and homes of the people. Pictures may show such scenes as a snow-covered mountaintop or a river and a tree. Japanese artists are especially well known for their water-color paintings, paintings on silk, and wood-block prints.

The Japanese learned the art of making wood-block prints from the Chinese. To make a wood-block print, a design is first painted by an artist. Then, skilled craft workers carve the design into wooden blocks—one for each of the colors in the painting—and make the prints on special paper. (See picture on page 103.) In the 1600's prints became popular among the common people of Japan, who could not afford to own original paintings. The early Japanese prints showed gods, beautiful women, or actors. In the early nineteenth century, landscape paintings became popular. Two of the finest artists of this period were Hokusai Katsushika and Hiroshige Ando. One of Hokusai's prints is shown below.

Literature. Japan has a heritage of fine literature. *The Tale of Genji*, written in the eleventh century, is considered one of the world's first important novels. Its author was Murasaki Shikibu, a lady in the emperor's court. This novel tells the story of a prince named Genji, and gives a beautiful and realistic pic-

ture of the way the people of the court lived.

Modern Japanese novelists include Yukio Mishima, Junichiro Tanizaki, and Yasunari Kawabata. Kawabata was the first Japanese to receive the Nobel Prize for literature. His best-known works include *Snow Country* and *A Thousand Cranes.* These stories have been translated into English and several other languages.

In addition to novels, the Japanese enjoy poetry. A popular type of poem in Japan is the haiku, which developed

Making wood-block prints is a traditional Japanese art. The picture at right shows a highly skilled craft worker carving a design in a block of wood. Next he will apply ink to the design and press a special kind of paper against it. Below is a wood-block print designed by the Japanese artist Hokusai (1760-1849). This print is one of a series of thirty-six views of Mt. Fuji. What do you think Hokusai was trying to show in this picture?

in the seventeenth century. A Japanese haiku has three lines and seventeen syllables. In these few lines, however, the reader sees and feels a great deal. Here is an example of a haiku:

> The plum branches beat
> Against my window at night,
> Frightened by the wind.

People in Japan still enjoy writing this type of poetry so much that newspapers carry daily haiku columns.

The theater. Two important forms of drama created by the Japanese are Noh and Kabuki. Noh plays originated in the fourteenth century as entertainment for the upper classes. All parts of a Noh play, from the scenery and costumes to the words and movements of the actors, must follow formal rules. The chanting of a chorus is an important part of a Noh play.

Kabuki plays were developed in the seventeenth century to entertain the common people. They are more popular than the Noh plays, because they are easier to understand. In a traditional Kabuki play, men perform both men's and women's roles.

Kabuki actors sing, dance, and speak their lines while music is played in the background. They wear heavy, elaborate costumes and mask their faces with thick makeup. Feelings such as anger, fear, and sadness are shown in exaggerated ways. For example, actors may stamp their feet, cross their eyes, or pose silently.

At first, the music you hear at a Kabuki play may sound unusual to you. But you will soon find that it makes an exciting background for the action on the stage. The musicians play instruments such as flutes, drums, gongs, and the samisen.* One of the most interesting instruments consists of two small blocks of wood. These are banged sharply on the floor whenever the action of the play becomes dramatic.

Sculpture. Another important form of traditional art in Japan is sculpture. For hundreds of years, Japanese artists have been making bronze and wooden images of gods, saints, and

A Kabuki play may seem unusual to Americans seeing one for the first time. How do you feel about something that is different from what you are used to? Do you assume that it must not be any good? Or do you try to understand it? How can people learn to appreciate the arts of a country with a culture different from theirs?

Culture

by Western artists are popular in Japan also. At the same time, the Japanese are creating new works of art that are enjoyed by people all over the world.

Crafts

Lacquer ware. At a village factory in the mountains of Japan, you can see lacquer ware being made. Craft workers are using wooden spatulas to spread sticky, black lacquer on trays made of cypress wood. After the trays are covered with the lacquer, they are placed in a cabinet to dry. They will be coated with more layers of lacquer and dried many times before they are finished. Each time a tray dries, it is smoothed with a rough stone called a whetstone. Some of the best lacquer ware is painted as many as forty times.

At the factory you can see many articles of lacquer ware that are finished. There are hairpin boxes, tables, and chests. Most of these are red or black in color. When you rub your fingers across a lovely red table, it feels as smooth as velvet.

Japanese craft workers have discovered several different ways to decorate lacquer ware. Graceful designs may be drawn on by hand or carved into the wood before it is lacquered. Sometimes fine silver or gold powder is sprinkled into the lacquer to give an article a bright, sparkling finish.

heroes. Some of these are very small. However, in Kamakura* there is a bronze statue of Buddha about forty feet high. (See picture on pages 74 and 75.)

Changes in Japanese arts. As you know, Japan opened its ports to foreign trade in the nineteenth century. It was not long before people in the West began to appreciate the beauty and importance of Japanese arts. Meanwhile, the arts of the Western world began to influence the Japanese. Today, many modern buildings in Japan resemble those in the United States and Europe. Symphonies, operas, plays, and books

Silk. In the section of Kyoto called Nishijin, men and women weave fabrics of silk on looms in their homes. Some of these craft workers weave gleaming silk threads into delicate gauze material. Others make heavy satins and brocades. Nishijin weavers make some of the loveliest silk in Japan.

Porcelain, cloisonné, and pottery. In a shop window in the city of Nagoya you see some beautiful dishes and boxes. To the left is a large, ivory-colored plate, decorated with a lovely design of red, green, blue, and gold curly lines. The creamy background of the plate looks as though it were covered with many tiny cracks. This is a piece of Satsuma porcelain, made by a fine craft worker on the island of Kyushu.

The jewel-bright colors of a tiny metal box catch your eye. This box took many months of patient hand labor to complete. First, thin, ribbonlike strips of silver were bent and fastened to the surface to form a raised design. Next, each of the tiny spaces between the silver strips in the design was filled with colored enamel. Then the box was baked, and patiently polished until its surface was as smooth as gleaming satin. Articles decorated in this way are called cloisonné.

Near the window is a row of pottery cups. These, too, were carefully made by hand. Although they are not delicately thin like the Satsuma ware, their pleasing shape and glowing colors make them very beautiful.

Dolls. To see some dolls created by Japanese craft workers, you visit a store in Tokyo. On the shelves are dolls made in many different parts of Japan. Dolls with clay heads, made in Kyoto, look so real that they almost seem alive. Several of the dolls are sitting on bent knees in Japanese fashion. Others seem to be dancing. The bodies of these dolls are made of wood and wire. Their arms and legs can be bent into many lifelike positions.

Much work and patience were required to make the costumes for these dolls. One is dressed in a soft, silk kimono. Another doll wears a Japanese

gown of purple brocade and holds a small paper parasol. Most Japanese dolls like these are made to be admired, rather than to be used as toys.

During a temple festival held in December, you see thousands of bright-red Daruma dolls for sale. These dolls are made by the members of farming families when they are not busy with their farm work. Daruma dolls, which always return to an upright position when they are tipped over, symbolize a person's ability to bounce back after misfortune. The people who buy the dolls keep them for a year and then bring them back to the temple to be burned in a special ceremony. New dolls are purchased for the next year.

Making Daruma dolls. These papier-mâché dolls are made by farming families when they are not busy with farm work. The dolls are sold at special fairs during shrine or temple festivals held in midwinter.

During the New Year's Festival, a girl plays a game called battledore and shuttlecock with her grandmother. Her brother plays with a kite. This festival is the most important national celebration in Japan.

11   Festivals and Recreation

The New Year's Festival. In the Japanese home you are visiting, you are awakened early in the morning on New Year's Day by the sound of clapping hands. The older people have risen early and are welcoming the rising sun by bowing to it and clapping their hands. Soon you hear the sounds of laughter and activity as the members of the family dress in their best kimonos.* Many of the children have new kimonos to wear.

When it is time for the first meal of New Year's Day, you join the family around a low table in the living room. At this meal you eat foods that are prepared especially for this holiday. One of them is a vegetable soup with rice cakes in it. After you finish eating, you go out with the family to call on friends and relatives. During these visits, presents are exchanged, much as they are at Christmastime in many other countries.

Offices and schools are closed today, and the streets are crowded with people. As you walk along, you see children flying their kites. You stop for a moment to watch a game of battledore* and shuttlecock.

Most of the houses you pass are decorated with objects such as fern

*See Glossary

leaves, oranges, or lobsters which represent good luck or good wishes for the coming year. Near the doorways are small pine trees to symbolize long life, and bamboo stems for virtue.

At home that evening, members of the family enjoy a card game called "Songs of a Hundred Poets." This game is traditionally played during the New Year's season.

The holiday officially ends January 3, but the celebrations continue until the middle of the month. One exciting event takes place on January 6. At this time, Tokyo fire fighters, dressed in costumes of long ago, march through the streets carrying banners and tall ladders. Some of them perform daring acrobatic tricks on the tops of the

Tokyo fire fighters dressed in costumes of long ago perform daring acrobatic tricks during the Japanese New Year's season.

ladders. The New Year's celebration is one of the happiest festivals in Japan.

Japan is a land of festivals. The Japanese people enjoy many other festivals throughout the year. Some are religious celebrations, which are held in honor of special gods. Others celebrate the blossoming of certain flowers or the coming of a new season. Christmas is also observed by many Japanese Christians and their friends.

The Doll Festival. Now it is March 3. On this day, Japanese girls entertain their friends and display special dolls. They dress in their prettiest kimonos and use their most polite manners.

As you enter a Japanese home, a little girl welcomes you. You kneel on a cushion, and she serves you diamond-shaped rice cakes and candies shaped like fruit. In one corner of the room you notice shelves covered with bright red cloth. Fifteen dolls dressed in the costumes of the ancient Japanese court are sitting on the shelves. Some of the dolls are very old and valuable. The little girl never plays with these dolls, but keeps them stored away all year until the time of the Doll Festival.

Social Needs

See pages 76-77

People in Japan celebrate many different festivals. For example, the picture at right shows fishers from Honshu celebrating the start of the fishing season. What are some of the other festivals and celebrations held in Japan each year? How do these festivals help people in Japan to meet their social needs? Do people in the United States sometimes meet their social needs in the same way? Give reasons to support your answer.

The Boys' Festival. On May 5, you notice paper or cloth streamers in the shape of carp flying from long bamboo poles outside many Japanese homes. This is the day of the Boys' Festival in Japan. The streamers swell in the wind and seem to swim like real fish. Carp

are fish that are able to swim upstream against strong currents. They represent strength and bravery to young Japanese boys who want to grow up to be courageous men. Boys also display dolls on this day, just as the girls do at their festival. However, boys' dolls represent ancient Japanese heroes and warriors. Miniature helmets, swords, banners, saddles, and armor are also displayed.

The Bon Festival. Imagine now that you are driving through a Japanese village on a night in mid-July. The streets glow softly from the light of paper

lanterns as well as from small fires before the entrances of homes. This is the first night of the Bon Festival in Japan, sometimes called the "Feast of Lanterns." It is the special time of year when Japanese people of the Buddhist* faith honor their ancestors. They believe that the spirits of their relatives who have died pay them a visit on these three days and that the lanterns and fires will light the way.

Usually on the last night of the festival, the young people in the village gather near the temple and dance the *Bon-Odori* until very late at night. They sing as they dance, clapping their hands and stamping their feet to the music of samisens* and drums. The Bon Festival is not a sad occasion, but a peaceful, joyful one. The Japanese Buddhist families rejoice that their relatives can be with them in spirit on these festival days.

The Seven-Five-Three Festival. On November 15, many shrines in Japan are crowded with boys and girls dressed in their best festival kimonos. All these children are seven, five, or three years old. The mothers and fathers have brought them here to express thanks that their children have reached these ages safely. They also pray for the future health and happiness of each child. This very beautiful celebration is called the Seven-Five-Three Festival.

Leisure-time activities. You have just joined a throng of happy-looking people on a crowded Japanese train. It is a holiday, and many of the family groups here are carrying picnic lunches and cameras. Some of these people may be planning to visit the beautiful lakes near Mount Fuji, or to spend the day in the gardens of some well-known shrine.* Others may be going to view the cherry trees that are in bloom at this season. The young people on the train are probably going mountain climbing. For the Japanese, one of the most pleasant ways to spend leisure time is to enjoy the beauty of their country.

The people who stayed in the city today are enjoying themselves in a number of different ways. Some are at home watching television, reading, or working in their gardens. Others are at skating rinks,

Rules
and
Government

See page 161

Baseball is a leading form of recreation in Japan. What are some reasons why people enjoy the game of baseball? Can you imagine playing baseball or any other game without rules? Are you glad you live in a community that has rules? Why? Why not? Discuss your answers to these questions with your classmates.

112

bowling alleys, or recreation parks. Still others are going to the movies or to Kabuki plays.

Sports. The Japanese enjoy many kinds of sports. In both the city and the country, you see children and adults playing baseball. An American schoolteacher taught some Japanese students to play this game about one hundred years ago, and today it is one of the most popular sports in Japan. High schools and colleges have baseball teams, and there are two professional leagues in the country. There is even a Japanese World Series.

Baseball is a borrowed game, but Japan has another spectator sport, just as popular, that is native to the country. This is a form of wrestling called sumo. Frequently, sumo matches appear on television. However, you probably would find it more interesting to visit the stadium and see the wrestlers in person.

You are now approaching the stadium where the sumo matches will be held tonight. At the entrance to the stadium are dozens of fluttering flags. The names of the wrestlers are written on the flags in large, picturelike symbols.

When you enter the stadium, you see a sand-covered platform topped with a canopy. This is the ring in which the wrestlers will test their strength and skill.

As you take your seat on one of the straw mats arranged around the platform, two huge wrestlers come into the ring. Proudly they show off their bulging muscles and strong, thick legs. Now the match begins. The wrestlers grip each other and push and twist and pull. Within just a few minutes, one man has forced the other outside the ring and has won the match. The champion bows his head in attention as the referee announces the outcome of the match. Then the two wrestlers leave the ring, and two other wrestlers enter.

In addition to sumo and baseball, the Japanese enjoy many other types of athletics. Two of these are judo and kendo. The sport of judo developed from an ancient Japanese method of self-defense. Kendo is the Japanese form of fencing. Some other sports enjoyed in Japan are volleyball, golf, table tennis, and swimming. During the winter, trains are crowded with people on their way to the ski slopes.

Japanese athletes take part in national and international competitions. Each year, thousands of amateur athletes from all parts of the country participate in the National Sports Festival. Japan was the host country for the Summer Olympics in 1964 and the Winter Olympics in 1972.

Kendo is the Japanese form of fencing. Instead of using swords, the contestants in a kendo match try to strike each other with bamboo poles. They protect themselves by wearing padded vests, long trousers, heavy mittens, and steel masks that look somewhat like the ones used by baseball catchers. What athletic abilities do you think a person would need in order to succeed at kendo?

Use Your Imagination

The Japanese people celebrate many festivals throughout the year. Imagine that you are a visitor in Japan and have attended one of the festivals listed below.

New Year's Festival Doll Festival
Boys' Festival Bon Festival
Seven-Five-Three Festival

Do research in Chapter 11 and in other sources to find out how the Japanese people celebrate the festival you have selected. Then write a letter to a friend in the United States, describing the festival you attended. Explain the reasons for the festival, when it takes place, and how it is celebrated. The suggestions on pages 177-182, in the Skills Manual, will help you to find sources of information and write a good letter.

Explore a City in Japan

The cities of Japan are colorful, exciting places to visit. Imagine that a travel club has asked you to give an illustrated talk about one of the following cities.

Yokohama Kyoto Kobe
Nagoya Osaka Sapporo
Kitakyushu

Prepare a talk in which you provide information about the city's location, population, history, and points of interest. Then present your information to your classmates. Use a map and pictures or your own drawings to illustrate your talk. This book contains some of the information you will need. The suggestions on pages 177-179, in the Skills Manual, will help you locate additional information.

Adventures in Appreciation

1. In a library, find a collection of Japanese haiku and read several of these poems. Then select one haiku that you especially like. Draw or paint a picture that illustrates this haiku or that expresses the way you feel about it. You may wish to write out the haiku on one corner of the drawing.

2. Obtain a recording of traditional Japanese music and play it for your class. Listen carefully to the recording. It may sound strange to you because Japanese music uses a different musical scale than Western music. You may wish to play the recording a second time, so that you and your classmates will become more familiar with the different sounds of Japanese instruments. Then, as a class, discuss the following questions.
   a. How did this music make you feel?
   b. Did you like the music? Why? Why not?
   c. What ideas or feelings do you think were being expressed in this music?

The suggestions on pages 182 and 183 will help you to have a successful discussion.

3. Japanese flower arrangements follow a special pattern. Do research in other sources to discover how the Japanese arrange flowers and the meaning of these arrangements. Then prepare a flower arrangement in Japanese style and display it in your classroom.

4. With a group of your classmates, make a display of Japanese crafts. You may have objects such as lacquer bowls and Japanese dishes in your homes. Ask your parents if you may borrow these objects. Arrange the items in an attractive display in your classroom. Label each item in the display.

5. Find directions for origami, the Japanese art of paper folding or paper sculpture. Practice until you can make an origami object well, such as a bird or a fish. Then present a demonstration in which you teach your classmates how to create a simple paper sculpture.

6. Discuss this question with your classmates. Do you believe that an appreciation for music, painting, literature, and other arts can enrich your life? Give reasons for your opinions.

Think and Discuss

Family life is very important in Japan, just as it is in most other areas of the world. What makes the family such an important kind of community? Discuss this question with your classmates. In your discussion, you may wish to consider the following.

1. How does family life help people meet their needs?
2. How does family life influence the following:
   a. a person's feelings toward other people
   b. a person's attitudes toward his or her country and other countries
   c. a person's work and study habits

Division of Labor

See pages 163-164

These pictures show a Japanese farmer harvesting rice and a worker testing a radio in an electronics factory. Farming and working in a factory are two of the main ways of earning a living in Japan. Use the graph on the opposite page to find the percentage of Japanese workers who are engaged in these and other kinds of occupations. Then do research in other sources to discover the percentage of workers in the United States who earn their living in each of these ways. What similarities can you find between Japan and the United States? What differences do you find? What are some possible reasons for these similarities and differences?

Part 4
Earning a Living

Japan is one of the richest countries in the world. It produces more goods and services than any other country except the United States and the Soviet Union.

How has Japan become such a prosperous nation?

The chapters in Part 4 provide information that will help you solve this problem. In forming your hypotheses, consider how each of the following has affected Japan's prosperity:

- changes in farming methods
- the growth of industry in Japan
- trade with other nations
- the skills and attitudes of the Japanese people

See Skills Manual, pages 166–169

EMPLOYMENT IN JAPAN

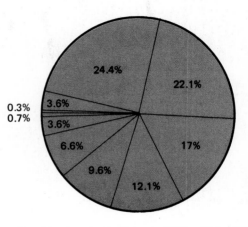

Manufacturing	24.4%	Construction	9.6%
Wholesale and Retail Trade and Finance	22.1%	Transportation and Other Public Utilities	6.6%
		Government	3.6%
Services	17%	Fisheries	0.7%
		Mining	0.3%
Agriculture and Forestry	12.1%	Other	3.6%

Total Japanese Labor Force in 1978 — 54.6 million

12 A Prosperous Country

Most people in Japan are fairly well off. They have enough food to eat and attractive clothes to wear. They also have some extra money to spend on luxuries—things that they want, but do not really need in order to live. For example nearly all of the homes in Japan have television sets, refrigerators, and washing machines. Automobiles are becoming increasingly common. Many Japanese families spend their vacations traveling through their beautiful country. Others, in increasing numbers, visit Europe and the United States.

Window shopping in Tokyo. In order to become a modern nation with a high standard of living, Japan has had to overcome a number of handicaps. What are some of these handicaps? What are some of the ways in which the Japanese people have worked to overcome these handicaps?

Another sign of Japan's prosperity is the fact that almost every family has money in a savings account.

What problems have the Japanese overcome to achieve prosperity? Japan's high level of industrial development and prosperity is an amazing achievement, for nature has given the people of Japan less to work with than it has given to some other nations. Most of the land in Japan consists of mountains, leaving only a small part of the country with land that is level enough for farms and manufacturing cities. There is less farmland per person in Japan than in most of the other countries of the world.

Japan also lacks many of the raw materials needed by modern industry. Most of the iron ore and nearly all of the petroleum used in Japan must be brought in from other countries. More than four fifths of the coking* coal and all of the bauxite* used in Japan must also be imported. In addition, Japan imports all of the raw cotton and raw wool used by Japanese textile factories. It is not profitable for the Japanese to use their limited amount of land to grow cotton or raise sheep. The small amount of farmland in Japan is used largely to produce food crops.

How do Japan's people obtain the food and raw materials they need? Japan has overcome the handicaps of little farmland and lack of raw materials for industry by becoming a manufacturing and trading country that serves as a workshop for other parts of the world. The Japanese buy raw materials from other countries. In the many factories of Japan, these raw materials are made into manufactured goods, which can be sold for more money than the raw materials cost. The money the Japanese earn by exporting manufactured goods is used to import more raw materials, food, and other goods.

If Japan were not a workshop nation, its people could not possibly live so well. Without manufacturing and foreign trade, millions of Japanese who now have jobs in factories and offices

*See Glossary

119

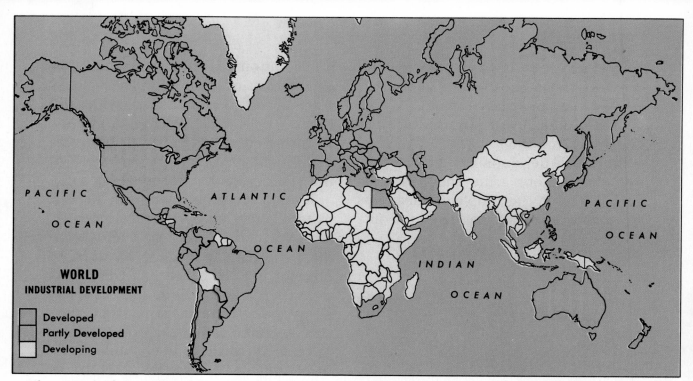

The spread of the Industrial Revolution. The world's most highly industrialized countries are generally referred to as developed nations. Countries in which the Industrial Revolution has as yet had little effect are said to be developing. In the partly developed nations, industrialization is well under way.

The Industrial Revolution

New ways of producing goods are developed. People in many parts of the world still live much as their ancestors did hundreds or even thousands of years ago. We in America, however, as well as people in certain other parts of the world, are living in ways that are very different from those of our ancestors. One main respect in which our lives differ from theirs is the way we produce goods.

During the seventeenth century, most goods were produced by people in their own homes or on farms. Work was performed mainly by the muscle power of human beings or animals, although a few simple tools and machines were in general use. Wind and waterpower were used for certain work, such as grinding grain.

Beginning about the middle of the eighteenth century, three important developments occurred in the way goods were produced. First, many new machines were invented to help people make things more quickly and easily. Second, steam and other new sources of power came into use. Third, factories were built to house the new machines. Together these three main developments, which all be-

gan in England, are known as the Industrial Revolution.

The Industrial Revolution spreads. The new ways of producing goods soon spread from England to other parts of the world. The United States, Belgium, France, and Germany were among the first countries to adopt the new methods.

The Industrial Revolution has continued to spread. Today, it is in different stages in different countries. In much of the world, industry is just beginning to develop. (See map above.) Most parts of Europe and North America are already highly industrialized.

Industrialization changes people's lives in several ways. For one thing, the standard* of living is generally higher in nations that have experienced the Industrial Revolution. Also, more of the people in such nations live in cities. The people in industrialized nations carry on more foreign trade than those who live in countries with little industry. They depend on people in many parts of the world for raw materials. They also depend on people in foreign countries to buy the goods and services that they produce.

*See Glossary

would have to work as farmers. Japan's small amount of farmland, divided among so many people, would provide each farmer with too little land to earn a living.

How did Japan become a prosperous workshop nation? Japan has been able to overcome its handicaps and become a prosperous nation largely because of the type of people and leaders it has. The Japanese are willing to learn, to make changes when needed, and to work hard for things they want. They are also a well-educated and highly skilled people. A short review of Japan's history shows how adaptable, capable, and industrious the people are.

Japan in the nineteenth and early twentieth centuries. When the Japanese opened their ports to foreign ships in the nineteenth century, Japan was still mainly a farming country. Most of its people were very poor. The Meiji* leaders, who came to power after Japan was opened, realized that the country needed to change. Many Japanese were sent overseas to observe and study, and foreign advisors were invited to Japan. Schools and factories were built, and by the early 1900's, Japan had become an important manufacturing country that depended on trade.

Japan in the early 1900's differed from the Japan of today, however. At that time, Japan's main exports were goods such as textiles and toys. Although some of the textiles were of high quality, toys and other similar items were often poorly made. Many of the goods for export were manufactured in very small establishments that paid low wages. Because most Japanese industrial workers in the early 1900's earned such low wages, they could not afford to buy many goods for their own use. Farm workers were also poor. Most of them were tenant* farmers who had to pay as much as one half of what they raised as rent to their landlords.

Japan in the earlier part of this century differed from today's Japan in another way. Its military leaders wanted to conquer other nations and establish an empire. As Chapter 4 explains, the ambitions of these leaders led Japan into World War II, in which the Japanese were defeated.

Japan after World War II. The occupation forces that landed in Japan after it surrendered in World War II found an exhausted and broken country. Japan's mines, steel mills, and factories were suffering from extensive damage, and production was very low. Its overseas possessions were gone, and most of its trading ships lay at the bottom of the sea. The future of Japan looked very dark at that time.

In the years that followed, it seemed that a miracle took place in Japan. By the early 1950's, Japan was producing as many goods as it had before the war. By the middle of the 1960's, Japan had become one of the leading nations of the world in total industrial production.

How was Japan able to make such an amazing recovery? The Japanese were able to recover quickly partly because they received outside help. Under the direction of the Occupation, the Japanese government carried out a land reform program that made it possible for most Japanese tenant farmers to purchase farms. (See page 131.) This change encouraged farmers to use better farming methods and to increase the amount of food they produced.

The United States also gave Japan financial aid and other forms of assistance to rebuild its war-torn industries.

Two other outside factors helped Japan to recover. During the Occupation, the United States took over the main responsibility of defending Japan. As a result, the Japanese did not have to spend large amounts of money on their own defense, and so they had more to spend in building up their industries. Also, the development of industry in Japan was hastened by the Korean War.* During this conflict, the United States spent huge amounts of money in Japan for supplies. This helped Japan to earn still more money to use in building up its industries.

Although the United States played an important part in rebuilding Japan, the largest share of the work has been done by the Japanese themselves. These hard-working, highly skilled people have made good use of the opportunities that have come their way.

The Japanese also have shown that they still can make changes to fit the world in which they live. Today, in the prosperous countries of the Western* world, people are willing to buy expensive products, such as high-quality cameras and television sets. To meet the challenge of this market, Japan has stopped being mainly an exporter of cheap and poorly made goods. Instead, it has become an exporter of products that are extremely well made.

The government and business leaders of Japan have worked together to make this change. Modern factories have been established to produce television sets, transistor radios, motorcycles, and other high-quality products. Inspectors hired by the government and by private industry check to make certain that the goods manufactured in these factories are of high quality. These products often sell for less than similar products made in other nations. This is partly because Japanese factories, with their up-to-date equipment, produce goods very efficiently.

A chain of changes. The change from making inexpensive items to making high-quality products has helped to bring other changes in Japan. Because the large, new factories with their modern equipment can produce goods very efficiently, Japan has more and better goods to export. With more to sell, Japanese manufacturers have been able to earn more money. This has made it possible for them to invest in improvements, to enlarge their factories still further, and to pay their workers higher wages. As the workers

Assembling air conditioners. At one time, Japan produced large quantities of cheap, poorly made goods. Most of these goods were exported. Today, Japan's modern factories manufacture expensive, well-made products. Many of these products are exported, but the Japanese people now buy a large share of their country's manufactured goods.

earn more money, they are able to spend more for clothes, television sets, cars, and other goods. In other words, there is a growing demand for manufactured goods within Japan. This has made it possible for Japanese factories to earn even more money and to expand still further.

As industry grows and wages rise, still another change is taking place in Japan. Many farm people are taking jobs in industry. Only about twelve out of every hundred workers in Japan now work in farming. Most of Japan's people live in or near cities and towns. Some of these urban people work in factories. Others work as teachers, doctors, bus drivers, clerks, or in other jobs that provide services.

A country that is planning for the future. Today, Japan is far more prosperous than at any other time in its history. And the Japanese people are planning for an even brighter future. Government and business leaders have worked together to make plans for the coming years. These plans describe what needs to be done to make Japan even more prosperous. However, they are only intended to be a guide. No one is forced to follow them.

Some problems Japan is working to solve. The Japanese have made great progress, but they still face a number of serious problems. As you have seen, Japan depends greatly on foreign trade to meet its needs. It must import raw materials and export manufactured goods. Sometimes Japan has trouble obtaining raw materials at a reasonable price or finding buyers for its manufactured goods. These problems are described more fully on page 146.

In spite of Japan's prosperity, some people here are unable to meet all of their basic needs. This is especially true of older people. Workers in most Japanese business firms are forced to retire when they reach fifty-five. Often they have little or no income afterwards. Japan's government has been supplying money and medical care to some of these people. It also provides them with social clubs, recreation centers, and low-cost housing. But much more needs to be done to help retired people in Japan.

Another reason why some Japanese find it hard to meet their needs is the rising cost of living. Each year, people have to pay higher prices for the goods and services they buy. This is known as inflation. It is a problem that Japan shares with many other countries of the world, including the United States. Experts do not agree on the exact causes of inflation, or on the best way to stop it. Today, Japan's government is seeking ways to stop inflation without hurting the growth of industry.

As you discovered in Chapter 6, urban areas in Japan have grown rapidly during the present century. Today, more than one third of Japan's people live in or near the industrial cities of Tokyo, Osaka, Nagoya, and Kitakyushu. (See map on page 87.) The crowding of so many people into these small areas has led to a number of serious problems. Among these are traffic jams, the pollution of air and water, and a shortage of good housing. The text on page 84 tells what one Japanese city, Tokyo, is doing to solve these problems.

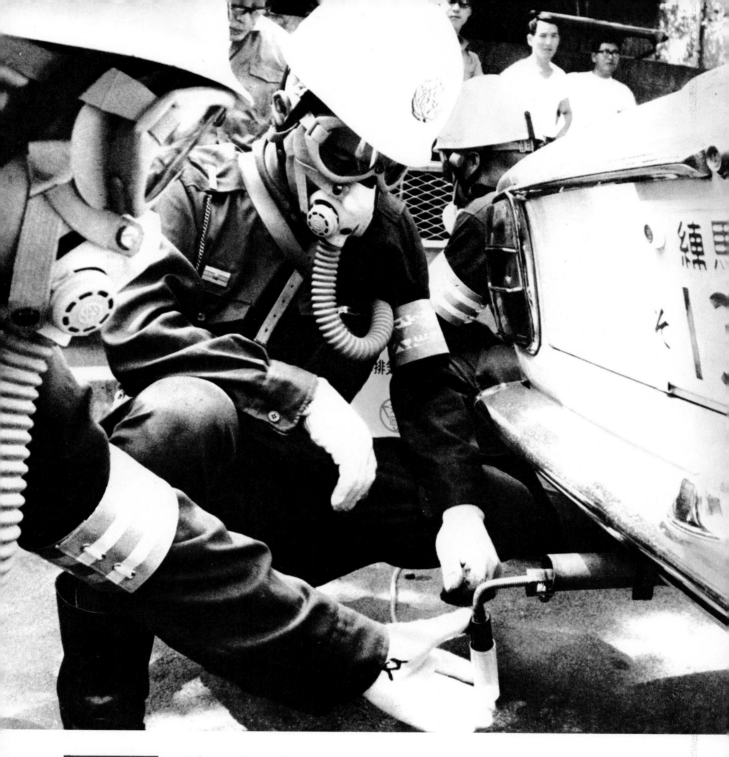

Ecology

Tokyo police officers checking the amount of carbon monoxide coming from an automobile's exhaust system. This is part of a program to try to reduce air pollution, which is harming the ecology of the Tokyo area. What is the meaning of the term "ecology"? What are some of the harmful effects of air pollution? What steps can be taken to reduce this kind of pollution? To answer these questions, you may wish to refer to the ecology entry in the Glossary and do research in other sources.

13 Farming

Japan has a shortage of good farmland. As you learned in Chapter 6, about 117 million people live in Japan today. To feed so many people, farmers must produce large amounts of crops. However, Japan is a small country with little good farmland. In fact, less than one sixth of the land here is suitable for farming. Most of Japan is too mountainous. In places that are level enough for growing crops, much of the land is taken up by towns and cities. These urban areas are growing larger every year. They are taking over more and more of the land that once was used for crops.

See page 163

Using Tools

A modern rice-harvesting machine. In recent years, the use of farm machinery has increased greatly in Japan. What facts help to explain why this is so? Compare the harvesting machine shown in this picture with the one shown in the left-hand picture on page 116. Which type of machine do you think would be used more often in Japan? In our country? Why do you think as you do? The information provided in this chapter will help you to answer these questions.

Farmers in Japan make good use of their land. Since farmland is so scarce, Japanese farmers try to use it as carefully as possible. Even hillsides and lower mountain slopes are used for farming. Level fields have been made on these slopes by building terraces. (See picture on pages 128 and 129.) To grow more and better crops, Japanese farmers use large amounts of fertilizer. Chemicals are used to kill weeds and insects. Also, farmers grow those crops that are best suited to the weather and soil in their area.

By using their land wisely, Japanese farmers are able to produce about three fourths of the food their country needs. The rest is bought from other countries, such as the United States.

A visit to a farm in central Japan. One warm, rainy morning in June, you stand at the edge of a small, flooded field on a farm in central Japan. This small, well-fertilized field is called a seedbed. Several weeks ago, rice seeds were sown here. Now the young rice seedlings are almost a foot high. They look like blades of bright-green grass growing close together.

The owner of the farm tells you that the rice seedlings are now ready to be transplanted into a larger irrigated field nearby called a "paddy." You ask why the seedlings were not planted in the paddy in the first place. The farmer explains that tiny new plants do not need much room in which to grow. While the rice seeds are sprouting close together in the seedbed, another crop

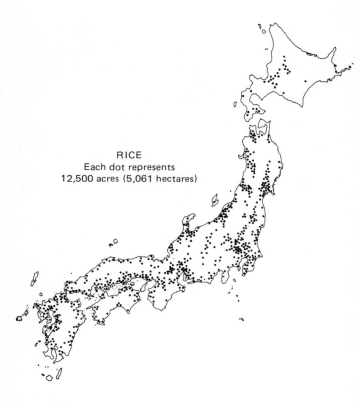

RICE
Each dot represents
12,500 acres (5,061 hectares)

Using
Natural
Resources

See pages 162-163

Terraced rice paddies. Why do Japanese farmers build terraces on hillsides and lower mountain slopes? What are some other ways in which natural resources such as land and climate affect farming in Japan? Do you think Japanese farmers make good use of the natural resources that are available to them? Explain why you think this.

Using a machine to transplant rice. Rice is Japan's most important crop. Japanese farmers are able to produce about four times as much rice per acre as farmers in India, which is a major rice-producing country. Why do you suppose this is so?

such as wheat can be ripening in the larger field. After this crop is harvested, the rice seedlings are transplanted into the larger field which has been flooded. In this way, the farmer is able to grow two crops on the same land each year.

Japan's farm products. In the farming area you are visiting, as in other farming areas of Japan, the level fields on the lowland and the terraced slopes are planted in rice. Rice produces a larger crop when it is raised in flooded fields, and only level land can be efficiently irrigated. On the hillsides where it is difficult to bring water for irrigating rice, there are fields of potatoes, soybeans, and other vegetables. Small groves of peach, apple, or mandarin orange trees also grow on some of the hillsides. In a few places there are fields of mulberry bushes or neat rows of dark-green tea bushes.

If you were to visit here in the winter, parts of the countryside would look

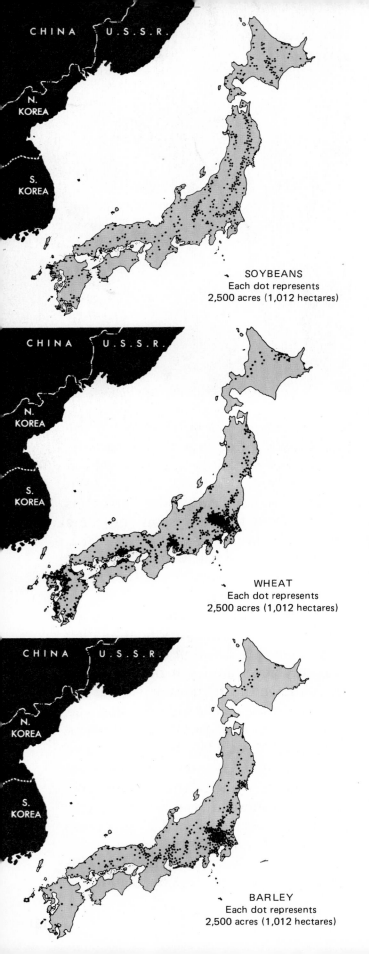

SOYBEANS
Each dot represents
2,500 acres (1,012 hectares)

WHEAT
Each dot represents
2,500 acres (1,012 hectares)

BARLEY
Each dot represents
2,500 acres (1,012 hectares)

very different. Wheat, barley, and other hardy grains would be growing on the terraced hillsides and in the drained paddy fields. In central and southern Japan farmers are usually able to grow crops in winter as well as in summer.

You do not see as many cattle or other kinds of livestock as you do in Western* countries. In Japan, as in other crowded parts of Asia, farmers have long used their small plots of land mainly to raise food crops instead of animals. They can obtain more food from each acre of land this way. In recent years, however, people have become more prosperous and have begun to eat more meat and dairy products. To satisfy the growing demand, more livestock are now being raised in Japan. Many farmers raise hogs and chickens rather than cattle, because these animals require less land.

On a tour of Hokkaido, you find that farming here is different in certain ways from farming on the other islands of Japan. There is more land for pasture here, and you see more cattle. Also, the rice raised on this island is a special fast-ripening type that can be harvested early in the autumn before the severe northern winter begins. In addition, you notice more farm machinery in use on Hokkaido.

Do many of Japan's people earn their living as farmers? About twelve out of every one hundred workers in Japan are farmers. Compared with the United States, where fewer than four out of every one hundred workers are farmers, this seems like a large part of the population. However, compared with most other Asian countries, where most of the people work in farming, it is a surprisingly small part. The number of

*See Glossary

A farm worker sorting mandarin oranges. In Japan, the amount of land planted in fruit crops has increased in recent years. As Japan's people have become more prosperous, they have begun to buy more fruit, meat, and dairy products.

farm people in Japan is becoming smaller all the time as more farm people are moving to towns and cities.

Do Japanese farm people earn a good living? Farmers in Japan are much better off than they used to be. Before World War II, most of Japan's farmers rented part or all of the land they worked. They had to pay as much as half of their harvest as rent to their landlords.

Under the Occupation* after World War II, a land reform program was carried out. The Japanese government purchased land belonging to landowners. Tenant farmers were permitted to buy this land by making payments over a long period of time. Today, about four fifths of Japan's farmers own all the land on which they work.

Most farm families in Japan have just as much income as city families do, even though the average farm is only about two and one-half acres in size. There are several reasons why this is possible. For one thing, modern agricultural methods enable Japanese farmers to cultivate their small plots of land very efficiently. Also, the government helps them by promising to buy most of the harvested rice at a good price.

Feeding silkworms mulberry leaves.

MULBERRY BUSHES AND SILKWORMS

Some of Japan's farmers earn extra money by raising silkworms. The main silkworm-raising area is in central Honshu. Because most silkworms eat mulberry leaves, farmers in this area grow mulberry bushes. Farm families spend a great deal of time picking the leaves, for silkworms eat continually until they are about five weeks old. At that time, they begin to spin their cocoons. From a small hole in the worm's lower lip comes a gluelike fluid, which quickly hardens into strong silk thread when the air touches it. The worm winds this thread around and around itself to form a snug cocoon. This silk thread is later unwound and used in making fine silk fabrics.

Until the 1930's, silkworm raising was one of the most important kinds of farming in Japan. Large amounts of silk were exported to foreign countries. Then many people began to use cloth made of synthetic fibers, such as rayon and nylon, in place of silk. The production of silkworm cocoons declined sharply. In recent years, however, there has been a growing demand for silk within Japan. As a result, silk production now remains fairly steady from year to year.

There is another important reason why farm families in Japan have good incomes. In almost nine tenths of these families, some family members work at outside jobs. Many of these people work part time at jobs in factories, on fishing boats, or in forests. Some farmers have small home workshops where they make parts for the electronics industry. Still others raise silkworms. (See feature at left.)

The use of farm machinery is increasing in Japan. Japanese farmers are using more farm machinery than in the past. As farmers earn more money, they generally are able to afford more farm machines. Also the use of farm machines is increasing because it is becoming difficult to find people to do hand labor as more and more farm people move to the city. The use of machinery is making Japanese farms more productive. Although the number of farm workers in Japan has decreased, the remaining workers produce more food.

One popular type of farm machine in Japan is the hand tractor, which can be used for a variety of jobs such as plowing and cultivating. Because it is not as large as the tractors used in our country, it is more practical for use on Japan's small farms. This machine can also be used to power threshing machines, saws, pumps, and other types of equipment. Using hand tractors, Japanese farmers can do as much work in one day as they once did in ten days.

Machines are also being used to do other kinds of farm work in Japan today. For example, hard jobs such as transplanting rice seedlings and harvesting rice were once done only by hand. In recent years, however, farm-machinery companies, experimental farms, and schools in Japan have worked together to develop machines that can do these jobs efficiently. Harvesting machines are being used on more and more Japanese farms, and rice-planting machines are also coming into use.

On the northern island of Hokkaido, the use of farm machinery is especially important. This is because farms on Hokkaido are large enough to make mechanization very profitable. Hokkaido has larger farms than the other islands of Japan partly because winters here are very cold and farmers can harvest only one crop a year. Hokkaido farmers must have more land in order to earn a living. Also, only about 5 percent of Japan's people live on Hokkaido, so there is more land available.

Preparing a rice paddy for planting. Japanese farmers are now using more farm machinery than they did in the past. What are some reasons for this change in farming methods?

14 Natural Resources

Japan has few natural resources. Many of the natural resources needed by modern industry are lacking in Japan. However, by making good use of the resources it has and by importing needed raw materials, Japan has become one of the world's leading industrial nations. Japan's natural resources include waterpower, forests, fisheries, and a limited number of minerals.

Waterpower

Waterpower is one of Japan's leading natural resources. Japan has abundant supplies of waterpower in its many swift-flowing streams. The plentiful rainfall and the steep hills and mountains in Japan help to explain why there are so many of these streams. Japan's supplies of waterpower are important to industry because they are used to produce electric power. Electricity that is made from waterpower is called hydroelectricity.

To see how hydroelectricity is produced, let's visit a power project on one of Japan's rivers. Behind the dam that has been built across the river, we can see a lake, or reservoir.* Enormous amounts of water are stored in this reservoir. In the power station at the bottom of the dam we see several huge machines called turbines. When a control gate in the dam is opened, water rushes downward through pipes and spins the turbines. Shafts leading from the turbines turn generators, which produce electricity.

*See Glossary

Using
Natural
Resources

See pages 162-163

A Problem To Solve
The picture above shows a thermal power plant in Japan. (See page 136.)
More than three fourths of Japan's electricity is produced in thermal power
plants. Hydroelectric plants supply the rest. During recent years, the number of power plants in Japan has been increasing steadily. Why is this so? In
forming hypotheses to solve this problem, you will need to consider facts
about: (1) manufacturing in Japan, and (2) Japan's standard of living.

See Skills Manual, pages 166-169

PRODUCING ELECTRIC POWER

Japan's need for electric power has increased rapidly in recent years. Today, nearly every home in Japan is supplied with electricity for lights and for operating household appliances. Factories in Japan also depend on electric power for running machinery.

There are two main types of electric power plants. One type is called a hydroelectric plant. It uses the force of moving water to produce electricity. (See page 134.) The other type is called a thermal plant. In a thermal plant, water is heated to make steam. The steam spins turbines that run electric generators.

Some thermal power plants burn mineral fuels such as oil or coal to heat water for making steam. Other thermal plants heat water by using nuclear energy. In the United States today, many people are opposed to nuclear power plants. They claim that these plants are highly unsafe. In Japan, however, the government is very interested in developing nuclear energy. This is because Japan lacks oil and other mineral fuels. With nuclear energy, a great amount of power can be produced by using just a small amount of uranium.

Until recently, it was much more expensive to produce electricity with nuclear energy than with oil. But the cost of oil has been rising so rapidly that this is no longer true. Japan can now produce electricity with nuclear energy almost as cheaply as with oil.

Today there are about twenty nuclear power plants operating in Japan. A number of others are being built. By 1990, nuclear energy is expected to supply about one third of Japan's electricity.

Mineral Resources

An industrial nation like Japan needs many kinds of minerals for producing manufactured goods and electric power. (See the special feature at left.) Japanese mines produce a number of different minerals. But most of the mineral deposits in Japan are small. To meet the needs of its industries, Japan must import large amounts of minerals each year.

Coal. Japan's leading mineral resource is coal. However, most of the coal mined in Japan is poor in quality. It does not produce a very hot fire when burned. The main use for this

Iron ore for industry. Japan's mines supply only a very small part of the iron ore needed by the nation's factories. As a result, large amounts of iron ore must be bought from other countries. What are some other minerals that Japan must import in order to meet its needs?

kind of coal is for fuel in thermal power plants. Only a small part of the coal mined in Japan is suitable for making coke,* which is needed in the iron and steel industry. (See pages 148 and 149.) Japan imports more than four fifths of the coking coal it uses. The main suppliers are the United States and Australia.

Most of the coal mined in Japan comes from the islands of Kyushu and Hokkaido. The coalfields on Kyushu have been mined for many years. These mines are in a good location, close to the main industrial area of Japan.

However, the better coal from the Kyushu mines is being used up. So the Hokkaido mines are becoming more important.

Japan's coal-mining industry faces serious problems. The coal deposits are small and widely scattered. As a result, mining is difficult and expensive. Often, Japanese mining companies cannot sell their coal cheaply enough to compete with coal brought in from other countries. When this happens, mines are closed down and many coal miners are left without jobs. To help meet the growing need for power in

Japan, the government has been taking strong measures to aid the coal-mining industry.

Oil. Japan has only small deposits of oil, or petroleum. Yet this mineral is very important to Japan's people. It supplies about three fourths of all the energy used in this country. Oil is burned as a fuel in power plants to produce electricity. (See page 136.) It is also used in making gasoline, petrochemicals,* and hundreds of other useful products.

Japan must import nearly all of the oil it uses. Its main suppliers are Saudi Arabia, Iran, and other countries in southwestern Asia. Some oil is also imported from Indonesia. Chapter 15 tells about the problem Japan faces in getting enough oil to meet its needs.

Iron ore. One of the most important minerals used by industry is iron ore. It is the main raw material used in making iron and steel. (See pages 148-149.) Japan's mines supply only a small part of the iron ore needed by the nation's factories. To meet its needs, Japan buys iron ore from Australia, India, and many other countries. It also imports scrap* iron and steel, mainly from the United States.

The Japanese are working hard to increase their supplies of iron. For example, they have been using new methods of iron mining. With these methods, they can obtain iron from ore that used to be considered worthless. The Japanese are also trying to get more iron ore from other countries. Japanese experts have traveled to many parts of the world searching for new deposits of iron ore.

Other minerals. Two minerals that are plentiful in Japan are limestone* and sulfur.* Most of the other minerals needed by modern industry are lacking in this country. For example, Japan must import nearly all of the tin and bauxite* it uses. Japan imports more than nine tenths of its copper and more than half of its lead and zinc. It also imports other metals that are mixed with iron to make high-quality steel. Phosphate rock and potassium salts are imported for use in making fertilizer. Large amounts of salt are imported also.

Forest Resources

Forests are an important resource in Japan. Forests cover more than six tenths of the land in Japan. These forests are mainly in the mountains, where the land is not suitable for farming. Because Japan stretches so far from north to south, its forests differ greatly from place to place. In the highlands of northern and central Japan are forests of evergreen trees such as pines. Both evergreens and trees that lose their leaves in winter grow in the lowlands of northern and central Japan. In the lowlands of the southernmost islands are broadleaf evergreen trees, such as camphor and live oak. Groves of treelike bamboo* plants grow in both southern and central Japan. The hollow stalks of bamboo plants are used in making baskets, fishing rods, and other useful articles.

Japan's forests are highly important to the people. The roots of the trees help to prevent the soil on the slopes from washing away during heavy rains. Wood is used for making charcoal, which is an important fuel in Japanese homes. Many houses and household articles are made of wood.

Loading logs in northern Honshu. Forests cover more than six tenths of the land in Japan. They are very important to Japan's people. Why is this so? What is Japan doing to maintain its forests?

Large amounts of wood are needed in industry. Japan is a major producer of plywood.* It also has many pulp and paper mills. To make pulp, wood is ground up or cooked with chemicals. Wood pulp is the main ingredient in making paper. It is also used in making many kinds of plastics and synthetic* fibers.

Japan must import much of the wood it needs. Even though Japan has large forests, it cannot meet its own needs for wood. Today, about two thirds of the wood used in Japan must be imported. Among the main suppliers of wood are the United States, Malaysia, Indone-sia, and the Soviet Union. In addition, Japan buys large amounts of wood pulp from Canada and the United States.

History helps to explain why Japan cannot meet its own needs for wood. In the past, people in Japan did not always take proper care of their forests. They often cut down trees without planting any new trees in their place. This caused serious damage to the forests. Today the Japanese government is carrying out a program of reforestation.* Even if this program is successful, Japan will probably still have to import wood to meet the growing needs of industry.

139

Fisheries

A visit to a Japanese fishing village. You are sailing across the blue waters of the Inland Sea near southern Honshu. Ahead of you is a small, green island. As you approach the island, you notice a small village along the edge of the sandy beach. Behind the village, the land slopes upward. On the lower part of the hillside are tiny farm plots. The rest of the slope is covered with trees and thickets of bamboo.

The narrow, sandy beach is lined with small boats, and fishnets are drying in the sun. Near the water, some of the villagers are digging in the yellow sand for clams. Farther along the beach, other villagers are building small straw fires beneath their boats. The smoke and fire will kill the barnacles* and sea worms that cling to the bot-

Preparing the day's catch of fish for market. Most of Japan's fishers live in small villages near the coast. These people generally are not able to earn a very good living. Why do you suppose they continue to do this kind of work instead of changing to other occupations?

toms of the boats. Nearby you see men and women mending nets.

Most of Japan's fishers live in small villages much like this one, and fish in waters near the coast. Many of them are self-employed, with their own small boats and fishing equipment, while others work for someone else. In general, these coastal fishers are not able to earn a very good living.

Many different kinds of food are brought in from Japan's coastal waters. Such fish as sardines, herring, and mackerel are caught with nets or with

hooks and lines. Long-armed octopuses* are trapped in special pots. Along some of Japan's island coasts, large quantities of shellfish and seaweed are gathered. You can see this seaweed drying on racks near many fishing villages. It is used in making various foods.

Modern company-owned vessels bring in most of Japan's fish catch. Today most of Japan's total fish catch is brought in by modern fishing vessels, owned by companies rather than individuals. These modern, company-owned ships are able to go far out to sea. Some of them stay in the home waters of Japan. Others go to distant fishing grounds near Africa, South America, and other parts of the world.

To see some of Japan's modern fishing vessels, you visit one of the many harbors along the coast. Anchored here is a fleet of ships that have just returned from a three-month fishing trip on the Pacific Ocean. These ships carry huge nets that are used to catch large quantities of salmon. Other deep-sea ships bring in catches of crab, tuna, and other seafood. Still others search the Antarctic Ocean and the northern Pacific for whales.

You wonder how fish are kept from spoiling on the ships that go so far from home. A man nearby explains to you that some fleets of deep-sea vessels are accompanied by large "factory ships." Each day's catch is cleaned and canned aboard these factory ships. On other deep-sea ships, the fish are refrigerated and unloaded at foreign ports. For example, one large fleet of Japanese fishing boats catches tuna and other fish in the Atlantic Ocean and unloads them at ports in western Africa.

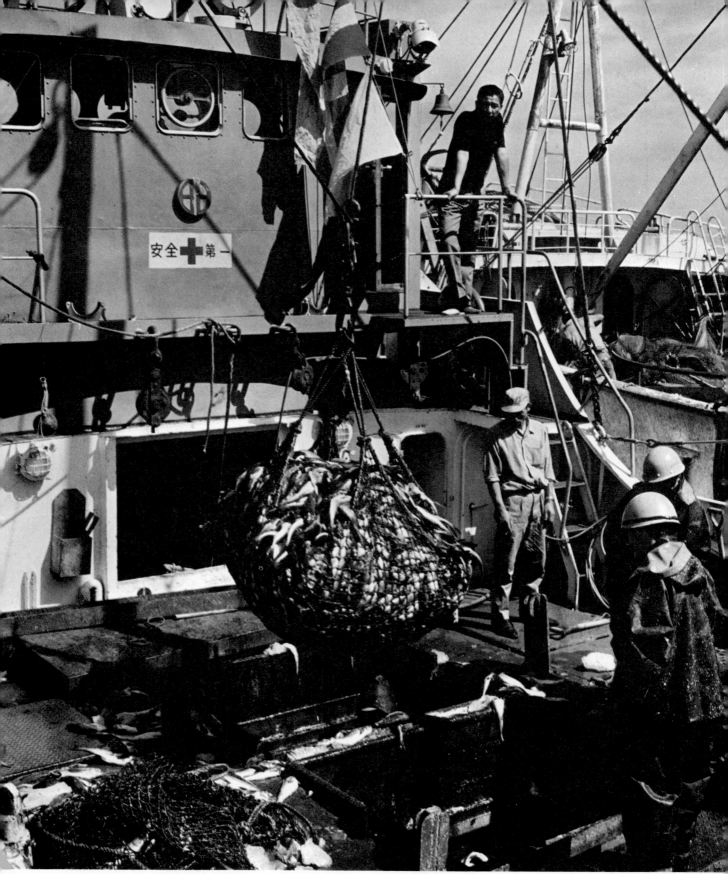

Unloading fish from an oceangoing ship. Japan is one of the world's leading fishing nations. Why is fishing so important in Japan? What major problem does Japan's fishing industry face?

Fishing is important to Japan. For many years, Japan has been one of the world's leading fishing nations. Fishing is important to the Japanese for several reasons. The waters around this island nation contain some of the world's best fishing grounds. For centuries, fish have been the main source of protein* in the diet of Japan's people. This is partly because meat has been scarce in Japan, while fish are plentiful. Fish have other uses also. For example, they are used in making fish oil and certain kinds of fertilizer. By selling fish to other countries, Japan earns money to buy goods it cannot produce itself.

Problems of Japan's fishing industry. Today, Japanese fishers are having trouble finding enough fish to catch. The waters near the coast of Japan do not produce as many fish as they did in the past. This is largely because of water pollution. (See page 84.) In recent years, many nations have claimed the right to control all fishing within about two hundred miles of their coasts. The best fishing grounds are located in these coastal areas. Sometimes, Japanese fishers must pay large sums of money to use these fishing grounds. At other times, they are not allowed to fish there at all. To help solve this problem, Japan is sending research teams to find new fishing grounds in other parts of the world.

Problems also face Japanese whale hunters. So many whales have been killed throughout the world that some kinds are in danger of dying out. For this reason, some people are calling for a worldwide ban on whale hunting. Such a ban would be harmful to Japan, since its whaling industry is among the world's largest.

CULTURED PEARLS

One of the interesting branches of Japan's fishing industry is the cultivation of pearls. To learn about pearl culture, we travel to the pearl farms along the coast of Ise Bay in central Japan. (See map on page 25.) Several girls are diving for oysters in the bay. These oysters are used to produce pearls. They are kept in cages anchored to rafts in the bay until they are about three years old. Then they are taken to a nearby plant. There, each oyster's shell is carefully opened by a skilled worker, and a tiny bead of mollusk* shell is placed inside. Then the oyster is put back in its underwater cage. The bead inside the oyster's shell irritates the shell lining, causing it to give off a smooth, lustrous substance called nacre. The bead is coated with layer after layer of nacre, and after about four years a beautiful pearl is formed. Pearls produced in this way are called cultured pearls.

The Japanese perfected the art of producing cultured pearls in the 1920's. Before that time, people depended on pearls produced by chance. These were very difficult to find. Today, nearly all the cultured pearls in the world come from Japan.

Pearl divers. These women dive for oysters that are used to produce cultured pearls.

Workers in an automobile plant. Japan is one of the world's leading industrial nations. Goods manufactured here include steel, motor vehicles, chemicals, and electronic products.

15   Industry

A Great Industrial Nation

Japan is one of the world's leading industrial nations. It is the world's largest producer of ships and the third largest producer of steel. It is also a leading producer of cars, television sets, cameras, and textiles. The Japanese buy many of the products their factories make. Japan also sells huge amounts of manufactured goods to foreign countries. Chapter 12 discusses how Japan became such an important industrial country.

Where are Japan's factories located? The map on the opposite page shows the location of Japan's main industries. There are factories in almost all parts of the country. However, one area has more industry than all the others. This main industrial area stretches like a long belt from central Honshu into northern Kyushu. Three fourths or more of the products manufactured in Japan are made here.

There are several reasons why most of Japan's factories are located in the main industrial belt. There are good

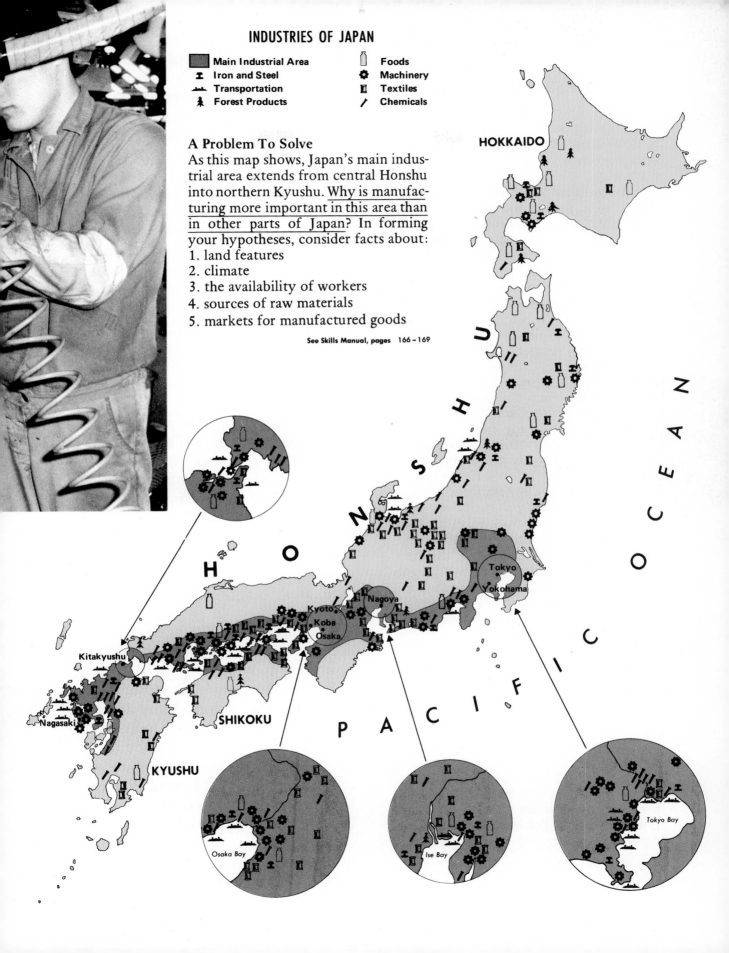

INDUSTRIES OF JAPAN

Main Industrial Area
⊥ **Iron and Steel**
⊥⊥ **Transportation**
🌲 **Forest Products**

Foods
⚙ **Machinery**
Textiles
/ **Chemicals**

A Problem To Solve

As this map shows, Japan's main industrial area extends from central Honshu into northern Kyushu. Why is manufacturing more important in this area than in other parts of Japan? In forming your hypotheses, consider facts about:

1. land features
2. climate
3. the availability of workers
4. sources of raw materials
5. markets for manufactured goods

See Skills Manual, pages 166–169

HOKKAIDO

H O N S H U

Tokyo
Yokohama

Kyoto
Kobe
Osaka

Nagoya

Kitakyushu

Nagasaki

SHIKOKU

KYUSHU

P A C I F I C   O C E A N

Osaka Bay

Ise Bay

Tokyo Bay

WORKERS AND EMPLOYERS

One reason why Japanese industry has been so successful is that most workers there are very loyal to their employers. Let us see why this is so.

In Japan, it has long been the custom for companies to protect and take care of their workers. Japanese companies give their employees a variety of benefits. For example, most companies pay workers a cash bonus twice a year. Many of them also provide low-cost housing for employees. Sometimes companies run stores where workers can buy the things they need at bargain prices. Many larger companies also provide their employees with recreation programs and medical care.

Workers in large companies usually get more benefits than workers in small ones. This is mainly because the larger companies have more money to spend on their employees. However, many small companies are finding it hard to attract young workers. They are being forced to give more benefits to encourage people to work for them.

In Japan, it is the custom for workers to stay with one company all their lives. Companies seldom fire any workers, or lay them off when business is bad. The custom of hiring people "for life" has some disadvantages. For instance, it may cause employers to keep people who are not doing their full share of the work. This, in turn, makes it harder for capable people to move into better-paying jobs. On the other hand, companies do not have to spend so much money training new employees all the time. Also, when workers expect to stay with the same company for a long time, they often develop strong feelings of loyalty to their employers.

Japanese employees are noted for their hard work and enthusiasm. They are seldom absent from their jobs. And they take a great deal of pride in their work. Although Japan has many unions, there are few strikes or other labor problems. These facts help to explain why Japanese factories are able to produce so many high-quality goods.

harbors here, and lowlands where the land is level enough for farms and cities. Also, the climate here is more pleasant than in some other parts of the country. As a result, a number of great cities have grown up in this area. In these cities, there are many people to work in industry and to buy the goods that factories make. Some of the cities in the main industrial belt are important seaports. Ships bring raw materials to these ports and carry away manufactured goods.

What problems does Japanese industry face? Although Japan's industry is still growing, it faces certain problems. The most serious problems result from Japan's need to import raw materials and export manufactured goods. (See Chapter 12.)

Sometimes the raw materials that Japan must import are scarce and expensive. As you have learned, Japan buys most of its oil from countries in southwestern Asia. In 1973, these countries cut off most of their oil shipments to Japan and other industrial nations. When the shipments began again, the price of oil was four times as high as before. In Japan, oil is the main fuel used in producing electric power. (See page 136.) Therefore, the jump in oil prices caused the price of electricity to rise also.

This "energy crisis" hurt the growth of industry in Japan. Many factories had to pay so much for electricity to run their machines that they could no longer make a profit. Today, the price of imported oil is still rising. And there is always a danger that the supply will be cut off again.

Industry also suffers if there are not enough buyers for manufactured products. For example, shipyards in

Constructing a giant tanker at Nagasaki. Japan leads the world's nations in shipbuilding. The Japanese have been able to accomplish this partly because they use special tools and methods that greatly reduce the time and costs needed for building a ship. Do research in other sources about shipbuilding. Then share your discoveries in an oral or written report.

Japan used to build many oil tankers every year. After the oil crisis began, foreign oil companies stopped buying new tankers. As a result, some Japanese shipyards had to close down.

Products of Industry

Iron and steel. One of the most important industries in Japan today is the manufacture of iron and steel. Japan produces more steel than any other country except the United States and the Soviet Union. Much of this steel is used by Japanese factories in making hundreds of different products. The rest is exported to other countries.

Japan lacks some of the raw materials needed for steelmaking. (See the special feature below.) However, the Japanese have overcome this handicap. They shop all over the world for the best coal and iron ore at the lowest possible price. To make good use of these imported raw materials, the Japanese have built some of the world's largest steel plants. These plants are equipped with the latest kinds of machinery. They use modern methods of steelmaking, such as the basic oxygen process. (See below.) With good raw materials and modern equipment, the Japanese can produce steel more efficiently than most other nations.

Other metals. Iron and steel are not the only metals produced in Japanese factories. Japan is also one of the

JAPAN'S IRON AND STEEL INDUSTRY

Japan is one of the world's leading iron and steel producers. This is an amazing fact, when you consider that Japan is poorly supplied with iron ore and coking* coal. These are two of the basic raw materials needed in making iron and steel. Nearly all of the iron ore and more than four fifths of the coking coal used in Japan must be imported. Japan does have a plentiful supply of limestone,* another raw material needed for steelmaking.

Iron is made by heating iron ore, coke,* and limestone together in a blast furnace. A strong blast of hot air is blown into the furnace. This makes the coke burn with a very high heat, melting the iron ore. As the iron ore melts, the limestone combines with some of the waste materials in the mixture. It forms a substance called slag. This rises to the top of the furnace, while the molten, or melted, iron settles at the bottom.

To make steel, the impurities in the molten iron must be burned out. This can be done in several different ways. About four fifths of Japan's steel is produced by a fast, modern method called the basic oxygen process. First, scrap steel and molten iron are put into a special furnace. Then oxygen is blown into the furnace through a tube at a very high speed. The oxygen helps to burn out impurities in the molten metal. Limestone is also added to the mixture to help separate the impurities. Later, the furnace is tilted and the molten steel is poured

A control booth in a Tokyo steel plant.

world's leading producers of aluminum, copper, lead, and zinc. These metals, too, are made from ores that Japan imports from other countries.

Machinery. Large amounts of steel and other metals produced in Japan are used in making machinery. Some Japanese companies make spinning and weaving machines for textile mills. Others produce huge generators* for electric power plants. Machines that cut, shape, and bore holes in metal are made in Japan also. These are called machine tools. They are used in making all kinds of metal products. Japanese factories also produce household appliances such as sewing machines, refrigerators, and vacuum cleaners.

One of Japan's fastest-growing industries is the manufacture of electronic goods. Japanese factories make transistor radios, television sets, tape recorders, and other electronic products for home use. They also make computers and other electronic equipment for factories and offices. Large amounts of electronic products are exported.

Transportation equipment. The making of transportation equipment is another important industry in Japan. As you have learned, Japan is the world's leading shipbuilding nation. Huge oil tankers and ore carriers are built in modern shipyards here. So are many smaller ships, including freighters and passenger liners. Japan's automobile industry

into a huge ladle. At this time, other kinds of metal may be added to the steel. Finally, the molten steel is poured into molds.

When the steel is solid but still hot, the molds are stripped away. The chunks of molded steel, called ingots, are heated again until they are an even temperature throughout. Next the ingots are sent to rolling mills to be made into bars. These are taken to finishing mills. There they are formed into sheets, tubes, and other shapes that can be used in making steel products.

Nearly one fifth of Japan's steel is produced from scrap iron and steel in furnaces heated by electricity. This way of making steel is usually quite expensive. So electric furnaces are used mainly for making special, high-quality steels, such as stainless steel.

Until recently, much of Japan's steel was made by the open-hearth process. Today, however, only a small amount is made in this way. Making steel by the open-hearth process usually takes about eight hours, compared with less than an hour for the basic oxygen process.

Molten metal being poured from a furnace.

149

Using
Tools

See page 163

A worker helping to build a train for the Shinkansen. (See page 154.) Do you think Japan could produce industrial products such as trains without the use of modern machines and tools? Explain your answer. Do you think the people of Japan could have the standard of living they enjoy today if they did not use modern machines? Give reasons for your answer.

has grown rapidly in recent years. Today Japan and the United States are the world's leaders in automobile production. Names such as Toyota, Datsun, and Honda are world famous. Japanese factories also produce large numbers of trucks, motorcycles, bicycles, locomotives, railroad cars, and airplanes.

Other metal products. Japan makes a great many other products that have metal parts. Its optical goods, such as cameras and microscopes, are sold all over the world. Japan is also known for its fine watches and clocks.

Oil products. As you learned earlier, Japan is poorly supplied with oil, or petroleum. Even so, the making of oil products is an important industry here.

150

Japan has more than forty oil refineries. In these plants, imported oil is made into gasoline, fuel oil, and other useful products.

Chemicals. There are many chemical plants in Japan today. Some of them produce basic chemicals, such as ammonia and sulfuric acid. Others use these chemicals in making a wide variety of products, including medicines, soaps, dyes, fertilizers, and plastics.

During the last twenty-five years, Japan has been producing more and more petrochemicals.* These are used in making synthetic* fibers, such as nylon and polyesters. They are also used in making plastics and synthetic rubber. Japan is one of the world's top producers of synthetic fibers and plastics.

Textiles and clothing. For many years, the manufacture of textiles has been a major industry in Japan. Today, this country is still among the world's leading producers of yarn and cloth. Some of the raw materials used in Japan's textile mills must be imported. For example, Japan buys cotton from the United States and wool from Australia. Other raw materials for the textile mills are produced within Japan. As you have seen, Japanese chemical plants produce large amounts of synthetic fibers. Also, some Japanese farmers raise silkworms. (See page 132.) The silkworms spin cocoons made of silk thread. This thread is unwound and used in Japanese textile mills to make beautiful and high-priced silk cloth.

*See Glossary

A petrochemical plant. The manufacture of petrochemicals is a very important part of Japan's chemical industry. All of the country's major petrochemical plants are located along coastlines. Why do you suppose this is so? What are some of the products made from petrochemicals?

Inside a **Japanese textile mill.** Japan is a leading producer of yarn and cloth. What are some of the raw materials used by the textile industry? Where does Japan get these raw materials?

Some of the cloth made by the textile mills is sent to Japanese clothing factories. There it is made into suits, dresses, and other articles of clothing worn by Japan's people. The rest of the cloth is exported to other countries.

Food. The branch of manufacturing that prepares food for people to eat is called food processing. Since Japan has so many people to feed, it is not surprising that food processing is an important industry here.

For centuries, the main food in Japan has been rice. Other traditional foods include fish, tofu,* pickled rad-

ishes, and *miso** soup. Most traditional Japanese foods are processed in small shops that employ only a few workers.

In recent years, many new foods have become popular in Japan. Among these are bread, butter, cheese, milk, meat, and other foods popular in the West. Many flour mills, dairies, and meat-packing plants have been built in Japan. There are also factories that make beer and other beverages.

Some modern factories in Japan process foods for export to other countries. For example, there are plants that can or freeze tuna, crabmeat, and other kinds of seafood.

16 Transportation and Communication

Morning rush hour in a Tokyo train station. It is morning in a Tokyo train station, and you are being pushed along by a great crowd of people hurrying toward the train that will take them to work. The crowd is so dense that you could not turn back even if you wanted to. If you dropped a package or a shoe, you would not dare stoop down to pick it up for fear of being trampled. When you reach the train, there are no seats left, so you crowd against the other people standing in the aisle. On schedule, the doors close, and the train begins to move.

Train travel is an important form of land transportation in Japan. Each day, millions of people travel by train in Japan. The top map on page 155 shows that there is railroad service on all four of the country's main islands.

The mountains that cover much of Japan make it very difficult and expensive to build railroads. It has been necessary to build many tunnels through the mountains. Thousands of railroad bridges have been constructed across streams that flow down the mountain slopes.

In spite of the difficulties the mountains of Japan cause in building railroads, Japan has about 17,000 miles of railroad tracks. The most heavily traveled railways are in the industrial

A Tokyo train station at rush hour. Traveling by train is much more common in Japan than in our country. Why do you suppose this is so? Do you think train travel might have advantages over travel by automobile in large urban areas? Explain your answer.

area that extends from Tokyo into northern Kyushu. Trains that travel the main routes in Japan are run by a government-owned company called the Japanese National Railways. Some of the smaller railroad lines are owned by private companies.

In recent years, much has been done to improve railroad service in Japan. Steam locomotives have been replaced by diesel* locomotives and electric trains. Also, a high-speed railroad line called the Shinkansen has been developed. People can now travel on the Shinkansen between Tokyo and Fukuoka in northern Kyushu. (See top map on page 155.) Trains on this line sometimes travel more than 125 miles per hour. Other Shinkansen lines are being built to connect Tokyo with cities in northern Japan.

In Tokyo, Osaka, and several other large cities, many people travel by subway. Tokyo's subway system is the fourth largest in the world. It covers a distance of more than 170 miles.

Cars, trucks, and buses. Now you are riding a motorcycle down a busy street

*See Glossary

A high-speed train of the Shinkansen, passing by Mount Fuji. The trains of this line are powered by electricity. They can travel at a speed of more than 125 miles per hour.

A Problem To Solve

As the maps on this page show, a network of railroads, roads, and airways reaches most parts of Japan. Coastal and ocean-going ships also serve the country. Why is a good transportation network important to Japan? In forming your hypotheses, you will need to consider:

1. how Japanese factories get their raw materials
2. how farm products and manufactured goods are distributed to the people who use them
3. how people get from their homes to where they work

See Skills Manual, pages 166-169

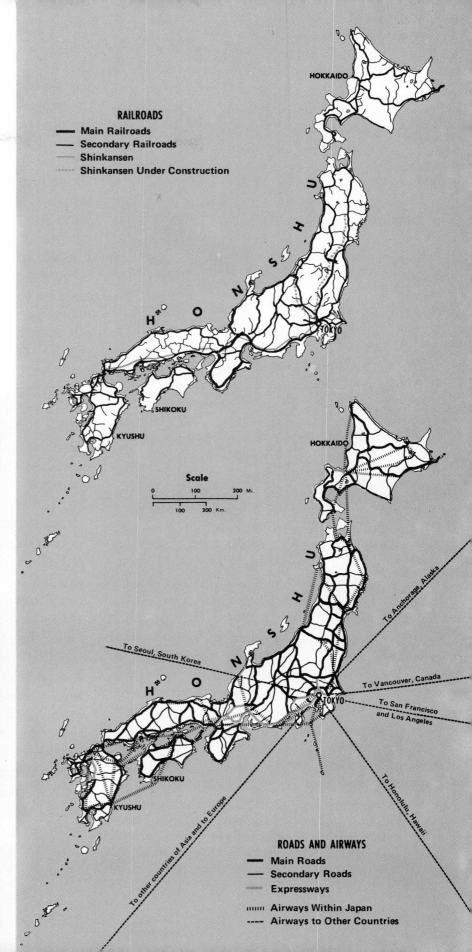

RAILROADS
— **Main Railroads**
— **Secondary Railroads**
— **Shinkansen**
···· **Shinkansen Under Construction**

HOKKAIDO

HONSHU

TOKYO

SHIKOKU

KYUSHU

Scale

0   100   200 Mi.

100   200 Km.

HOKKAIDO

HONSHU

To Anchorage, Alaska

To Seoul, South Korea

To Vancouver, Canada

TOKYO

To San Francisco and Los Angeles

SHIKOKU

To Honolulu, Hawaii

KYUSHU

To other countries of Asia and to Europe

ROADS AND AIRWAYS
— **Main Roads**
— **Secondary Roads**
— **Expressways**
···· **Airways Within Japan**
---- **Airways to Other Countries**

Modern expressways in Tokyo. The number of automobiles, trucks, and buses in Japan has almost tripled in the last ten years. To help take care of the increased traffic, the Japanese are building thousands of miles of expressways.

in Osaka. You have to move slowly, for traffic is very heavy. Sharing the crowded street with you are cars, trucks, buses, and taxis. The number of motor vehicles in Japan has risen greatly in recent years. As a result, there are often traffic jams in the larger cities. In some places, expressways have been built to help take care of the increase in traffic. But some people feel that these do not really solve the problem of traffic jams. They say the expressways merely encourage more people to drive cars into the cities. A better answer, they say, is for people to use buses, subways, and other means of public transportation.

Leaving Osaka, you travel into the countryside on a modern expressway. Roads like this one are rare in Japan. However, there are many two-lane roads that have been paved or surfaced with gravel to keep them from becoming muddy in wet weather.

You see many trucks on this expressway. In Japan, trucks carry much more freight than trains do. This is partly because trucks can often transport goods more quickly than railroads.

Now you turn off the highway onto a winding, unpaved mountain road. A crowded bus passes by, raising a cloud of dust. Before long, you pass a small three-wheeled motor cart. It looks somewhat like a motorcycle with a two-wheeled cart behind the driver's seat. Small motor vehicles like this have become common in Japan, for they do not cost much to buy or run. You pass some cars, but not as many as you would on an American road.

Each year, more freight is being transported by motor vehicles. Also, there is one automobile for every four people in Japan. Unfortunately, there are not enough good highways to carry this heavy load of traffic efficiently. The Japanese are working to solve this problem, however. They plan to complete about 6,200 miles of expressways by the year 1985. Some of these highways have already been built.

Air travel. On a trip to Tokyo International Airport, you see that it is a busy place. Every day, hundreds of planes fly in and out of this great airport. Some of the planes you see are from other nations, such as the United States and the Soviet Union. Others belong to Japan Air Lines. The planes of this government-owned airline carry passengers and freight to foreign countries as well as between cities in Japan. Other Japanese airlines also operate flights within the country. (See bottom map on page 155.)

Water transportation. Now you are touring the waterfront of the busy and important port city Yokohama. Anchored at the wharves are several giant freighters, which carry goods to and from foreign countries. Passengers are walking down the gangplank of a huge ocean

Passengers boarding a plane at Tokyo International Airport. The planes of Japan Air Lines carry passengers and freight to foreign countries as well as between cities in Japan.

Exchange

See page 164

A Problem To Solve

This picture shows goods being loaded onto a ship in Yokohama Harbor. Each year, ocean-going ships carry several hundred million tons of goods between Japan and other countries. Why is foreign trade important to the Japanese people? Discuss this question with other students. In your discussion, you may wish to consider facts about the following:

1. raw materials that are used by Japanese factories
2. how electric power is produced in Japan
3. markets for Japanese goods
4. farming in Japan

Other chapters in Part 4 provide information that will help you prepare for the discussion.

See Skills Manual, pages 166-169

liner. Many smaller ships and motorboats are steering their way carefully through the crowded harbor.

Yokohama is one of Japan's four main ports. The other three are Kobe, Nagoya, and Osaka. These port cities are very important to an island country like Japan. As you know, the Japanese people meet their needs by importing raw materials and exporting manufactured goods. (See page 119.)

Not all of the ships in Japanese harbors travel to and from foreign countries. Many of them carry goods from one Japanese port to another. Coastal shipping has always been important in Japan, because most of the people live on or near the coast. Today, water transportation is especially important for hauling bulky goods such as lumber and oil.

Communication. The Japanese people keep in touch with each other and with the outside world in many different ways. The government provides fast, efficient mail service. It also runs Japan's telephone and telegraph services. Japan has more telephones than any other country except the United States. Today, about 125 different daily newspapers are published in Japan. Radio and television stations broadcast news and entertainment to all parts of the country. Nearly all of the people in Japan have radios and television sets in their homes.

Keep Up With Current Events

Japan depends on its sale of exports to pay for the raw materials and power resources needed by Japanese industry. Therefore, trade relations between Japan and other nations are very important. Look for articles about trade relations between Japan and other countries in newspapers and magazines. Display these articles on a bulletin board in your classroom. As a class, discuss the significance of the events reported in these articles. The suggestions on pages 182-183, in the Skills Manual, will help you to hold a successful group discussion.

Make Discoveries About Rice

Rice is Japan's leading farm crop. Do research about rice in this book and in other sources. Then present your findings to the rest of the class in an oral report. Your report should include information about the following:

1. special conditions needed for growing rice
2. some of the ways rice is planted, cultivated, and harvested
3. some of the uses of rice

The suggestions on pages 177-182, in the Skills Manual, will help you to find information and to prepare your report.

Make a Minerals Chart

Prepare a list of the minerals mentioned in Chapter 14. Use encyclopedias or other resource materials to discover ways in which these minerals are used. Then, with the information you have gathered, make a chart that lists each mineral and its main uses. On the chart, indicate which minerals Japan produces in sufficient quantities to meet its needs and which minerals it must import. This could be shown in two different columns on your chart. You may wish to fasten pictures or samples of these minerals to your chart.

Investigate the Iron and Steel Industry

The iron and steel industry has helped make Japan an industrial power. Prepare a report about this industry, including information about the following:

1. the history of the iron and steel industry
2. the importance of steel in the modern world
3. the raw materials that are needed for making iron and steel
4. how iron is made in a blast furnace
5. the different ways in which iron may be changed into steel
6. different types of steel and their uses

You may wish to illustrate your report with pictures and diagrams. Refer to pages 177-182, in the Skills Manual, for help in locating information and preparing your report.

Think and Discuss

Discuss this statement with your classmates. Trade between different areas of the world helps people to enjoy a better way of life. In your discussion, you may wish to consider questions such as the following.

1. How does exchange between different areas of the world help people meet their physical needs?
2. How does exchange benefit industry?
3. Does exchange between different areas of the world help provide jobs? Explain your answer.
4. Can exchange help people in different areas of the world better understand one another? Why do you think as you do?

Make a Survey

During your study of Japan, you have discovered how important good transportation and communication systems are to the Japanese people. To find out how important good transportation and communication are to the people in your own community, ask some of your classmates to join with you in making a survey. Make appointments to interview the managers of several local stores. Ask questions such as the following.

1. Where were the goods sold in your store produced? How were they brought here?
2. Where do the workers in your store live? How do they get to and from work?
3. In what ways does your store advertise its goods? How important is advertising in obtaining customers?

When your survey is completed, evaluate the transportation and communication facilities in your community. How well do they meet the needs of the people who live there? In what ways might they be improved? Prepare a group report summarizing your conclusions.

Broadcasting a television program in Japan. In what ways do you think the people involved in producing a television program such as this one use the nine great ideas discussed in these pages?

Great Ideas

People have probably been living on the earth for more than two million years. During this long time, all people have met their needs in communities. They have found that only by living and working with other people can they have happy, satisfying lives.

In order to make community life successful, people have developed certain ideas and ways of living. We call these the "great ideas." Let us examine nine of these great ideas and see how they have made it possible for people to live in communities.

Cooperation. In every community, people need to work together in order to accomplish their goals. Working together is called cooperation. Long ago, when most people were hunters, they had to cooperate closely to protect themselves from wild beasts and to get the food they needed. In what ways is cooperation important to communities today? What are some of the ways in which people cooperate with each other? What might happen to a community if people were not willing to work together?

Rules and government. Every community needs rules to guide the ways in which people act toward one another. Why is this true? What kinds of rules does your own community have? How do these rules make life safer and more pleasant for everyone? What would it be like to live in a community in which no one obeyed the rules?

In every community, there must be a person or a group of persons to make the rules and see that they are carried out. In other words, all communities need some form of government. In what ways are all governments alike? How do governments differ from each other?

A police officer directing traffic on a busy street in Tokyo. Do you think a very large community like Tokyo needs more rules than a village or other small community? Give reasons for your answer. Do you think it is more difficult to govern a large community than a small one? Explain your answer.

Japanese students in a vocational-training class. Do you believe it is important for a community to provide opportunities for young people to learn job skills? Why do you think this?

Language. In order to live and work together, people must be able to express their ideas and feelings to one another. The most important ways of communicating are by speaking and writing. Scientists believe that all human beings—even those who lived in earliest times—have had some form of spoken language. Writing was not developed until about five thousand years ago.

How does language help you to meet your needs? What would you do if you could neither speak nor write? Would you be able to think and to solve problems without using language? Explain.

Education. Another great idea is education. In every community, the older people pass on certain ideas and skills to the younger people. Would it be possible to have a successful community without education? Why? Why not?

In early times, parents taught their children most of the things they needed to know in order to live successfully. Today, children in most parts of the world obtain a large part of their education in school. Do you think education is important for every person? Why do you think as you do?

Using natural resources. In order to meet their needs, people in all communities make use of soil, water, air, sunshine, wild plants and animals, and minerals. These gifts of nature are called natural resources. Would people be able to meet their needs for food, clothing, and shelter without using natural resources? Why? Why not?

People who lived on the earth long ago knew only a few ways of using natural resources to meet their needs. Today, we use hundreds of natural resources in many different ways. How have people's lives been affected by changes in the use of natural resources? How have changes in the use of natural resources affected your life?

Using tools. A tool is anything that people use to help them do work. What kinds of tools do you use every day? In all communities, people use tools to help them meet their physical needs. Would it be possible to have a successful community without tools? Why do you think this?

Tools that have a number of moving parts are called machines. Three hundred years ago, most machines were very simple. Then people began to develop more complicated machines. These could do many jobs that had formerly been done by hand. Today people use many different kinds of machines to produce goods. How do modern machines help people to meet their needs more successfully?

Division of labor. In every community, not all the people do exactly the same kinds of work. Instead, they work at different jobs. For example, some people earn their living by farming. Others work in factories or in offices. Dividing up the work of a community among people who do different jobs is known as division of labor.

By using division of labor, people are able to obtain more goods than they could if they tried to meet all of their needs by themselves. Why do you think

An office worker using a calculating machine. Do you think that life is easier for people who use modern machines than for people who use only a few simple tools? Why do you think this?

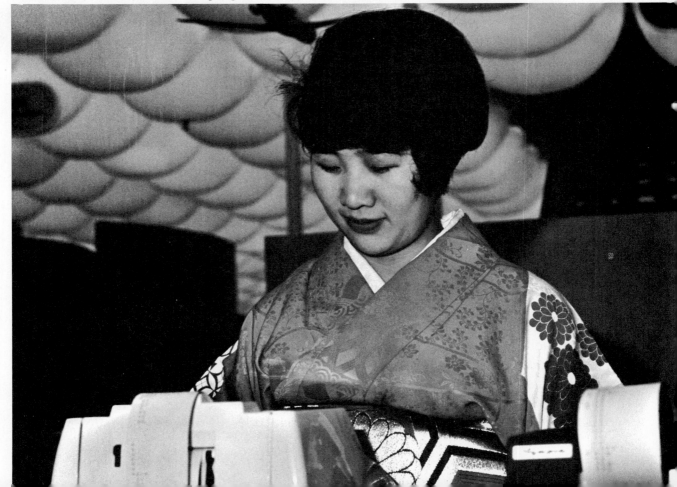

Shoppers in a Tokyo department store. How do you suppose these people got the money they need for making purchases? In what ways does the great idea of exchange help people meet their physical needs?

this is so? Would it be possible to have a successful community without division of labor? Why? Why not?

Exchange. Whenever people divide up the work of a community, they need to exchange goods and services with each other. In this way, they are able to obtain goods and services that they do not produce themselves. What would it be like to live in a community where people did not use exchange?

In early times, people did not carry on as much exchange, or trade, as people do today. We not only exchange goods and services within our own communities but we also carry on trade with people who live in communities far away. Do you think trade helps people everywhere to have a better life? Why do you think this?

Loyalty. In every truly successful community, most of the people are loyal to each other. They are loyal to the laws of their community and their country. They are also loyal to certain ideas and beliefs. In the United States, for example, most people are loyal to the principles of democracy. In addition, many people are loyal to their religious faith.

To what persons and ideas are you loyal? What are some ways in which you express your loyalty? How does loyalty help you to meet your needs?

SKILLS MANUAL

CONTENTS

Thinking and Solving Problems

Why the social studies are important to you. During the next few years, you will make an important choice. You will choose whether or not you will direct your own life. Many people are never aware of making this choice. They drift through life, never really trying to understand what is going on around them or why things turn out the way they do. Without knowing it, these people have chosen not to direct their own lives. As a result, they miss many enriching experiences. Other people make a serious effort to choose a way of life

A high school biology class in Japan. This classroom is equipped with several television sets so that lessons can be presented on TV. Do you think the students in this class must be able to think clearly and to solve problems in order to succeed in school? Will they need these abilities in order to be successful in the careers they choose to follow as adults? Explain your answers.

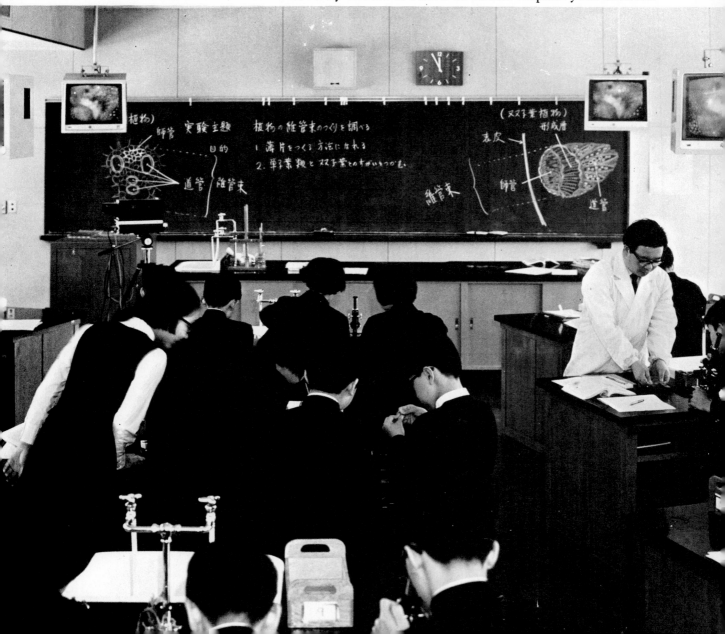

Thinking and the Three Types of Learnings

THINKING

One of the main reasons you are attending school is to develop your ability to think clearly. Thinking includes seven different thought processes. (See definitions below.) If you learn to use your higher thought processes, rather than simply repeat information you have memorized, you will achieve greater success in school and in life. In fact, your ability to fulfill your obligations as a citizen will depend largely on how well you learn to think. Your ability to think clearly will also help you make progress in the three types of learnings included in the social studies. (See chart below.)

Seven Thought Processes

1. **Remembering** is recalling or recognizing information.
2. **Translation** is changing information from one form into another, such as words into pictures.
3. **Interpretation** is discovering relationships among facts, concepts,* and generalizations.*
4. **Application** is applying the appropriate knowledge and skills to the solution of a new problem.
5. **Analysis** is separating complicated material into its basic parts to see how those parts were put together, how they are related to each other, and how the parts are related to the whole.
6. **Synthesis** is putting ideas together in a form that is not only meaningful but also new and original.
7. **Evaluation** is judging whether something is acceptable or unacceptable, according to definite standards.

THREE TYPES OF LEARNINGS

Understandings	Values and Attitudes	Skills
Concepts	Beliefs	Obtaining knowledge
Generalizations	Appreciations	Using knowledge
Facts	Ideals	Working with others

Understandings

You will truly gain an understanding of important concepts and generalizations when you use your thought processes to organize information in meaningful ways. In turn, the concepts and generalizations you develop will help you learn to think critically about new situations you meet.

Values and Attitudes

You will develop many constructive values and attitudes as you improve your thinking ability. Success in the higher levels of thinking will bring you faith that you can solve problems and make wise decisions. In turn, positive values and attitudes will help you to develop your thinking ability.

Skills

You will be more successful in developing the social studies skills when you use your higher thought processes described above. In turn, you will find that the social studies skills will help you do the critical thinking needed for solving the many difficult problems you will face during your lifetime.

*See Four Words To Understand, page 169

that will bring them satisfaction. If you decide to live by choice instead of by chance, you will be able to live a more satisfying life.

You will need three types of knowledge to live by choice successfully. Living by choice will demand a great deal from you. You will have to keep growing in three different types of learnings — understandings, values and attitudes, and skills. As the chart on page 167 shows, the type of learnings we call understandings includes the kinds of information you need in order to understand yourself, your country, and your world. The type of learnings we call values and attitudes deals with the way you feel toward yourself and your world. The third type of learnings includes the skills you need to use in gaining understandings and developing constructive values and attitudes. Among these skills are those you need for obtaining and using knowledge, and for working effectively with other people.

The social studies can help you grow in the three types of learnings. Your social studies class is one of the best places in which you can explore the three types of learnings. Here you can obtain much of the information you need for understanding yourself and your world. You can practice many important skills. Through many experiences, you can begin to evaluate what in life is worthwhile to you.

The problem-solving method will help you achieve success in social studies. Since the social studies are of such great importance, you want to use the best possible study method. You could just read a textbook and memorize answers for a test. If you did so, however, you would forget much of the information soon after the test was over. Your thinking ability would not improve, and you would not gain new, constructive values and attitudes. You would not have the opportunity to use many important skills, either. We suggest that you use a special way of studying called the problem-solving method.

You will want to use the problem-solving method as you do research. To use this method, follow these steps.

1. Do some general background reading in this book about a topic such as land, people, natural resources, or industry.

2. Choose an important, interesting problem that you would like to solve. Write it down so that you will have clearly in mind what it is you want to find out. (Look at the sample problem on the opposite page.) If there are small problems that need to be solved in order to solve your big problem, list them, too.

3. Consider all possible solutions to your problem and list the ones that seem most likely to be true. These possible solutions are called "educated guesses," or hypotheses. You will try to solve your problem by finding facts to support or disprove your hypotheses.

4. Test your hypotheses by doing research. This book provides you with four main sources of information. These are the pictures, the text, the maps, and the Glossary. To locate the information you need, you may use the Table of Contents and the Index. The suggestions on pages 177-180 of this Skills Manual will help you to locate and evaluate other sources of information.

As you do research, make notes of all the information you find that will either support your hypotheses or disprove them. You may discover that information from one source disagrees with information from another. If this should happen, check still further and try to decide which facts are correct.

5. Summarize what you have learned. Have you been able to support one or more of your hypotheses with facts? Have you been able to disprove one or more of your hypotheses? What new facts have you learned? Do you need to do further research?

You may want to write a report about the problem. To help other people share the ideas that you have come to understand, you may decide to illustrate your research project with maps, pictures, or your own drawings. You will find helpful suggestions for writing a good report on pages 180-182 of this Skills Manual.

You can use the problem-solving method throughout your life. In addition to helping you to achieve success in the social studies, the problem-solving method can help you in another way. By using it, you will learn to deal with problems in a way that will be valuable to you throughout your life. Many successful scientists, business executives, and government leaders use this method to solve problems.

A sample problem to solve. As you make discoveries about Japan, you may wish to solve the following sample problem.

> Throughout most of their history, the Japanese people have had to obey their rulers without question. Today, however, Japan has a democratic government. <u>What has made it possible for a people with little experience in self-government to govern themselves successfully?</u> In forming hypotheses, you will need to think about the following:
> a. the part that foreign nations played in bringing democracy to Japan
> b. the manner in which Japanese traditions prepared the people to be responsible citizens
> c. the standard of living in Japan
> d. the education of the average Japanese
> e. the news media in Japan, such as newspapers and radio stations, which provide the information that citizens need to make sound judgments about their government

The Index of this book will help you locate information that will be useful in solving this problem. You may also wish to do additional research in other sources.

Four Words To Understand

1. **A concept** is a big, general idea that includes many smaller, more specific ideas. An example of a concept is the idea of "trade." Many kinds of exchange are included in this idea. Two children who exchange marbles on the playground are carrying on trade. A person who pays money for a loaf of bread is also carrying on trade; so is a factory that buys raw materials from other countries and sells its manufactured products overseas. Only as you come to see the various things that the word "trade" includes do you grow to understand this concept. Another example of a concept is the idea of "climate."

2. **A generalization** is a general rule or principle that expresses a meaningful relationship among two or more concepts. It is formed by drawing a conclusion from a group of facts. For example, "Through trade, all people on the earth can have a better living," is a generalization drawn from facts about trade and the way people live in various parts of the world. It includes four concepts: "trade," "all people," "the earth," and "a better living." These have been put together to give a significant understanding about the world. The many facts you read about, hear about, or experience will make more sense if you think of them as statements that can be combined to form meaningful generalizations. Remember, however, that if a generalization is based on wrong or insufficient facts, or is carelessly thought out, it may be false. Make certain that you understand the concepts in a generalization, and judge carefully whether or not you think it is true.

3. **Values** are the things in life that a person considers right, desirable, or worthwhile. For instance, if you believe that every individual is important, we may say that one of your values is the worth of the individual.

4. **Attitudes** are the outward expression of a person's values. For example, if you truly value the worth of every individual, you will express this value by treating everyone you meet with consideration.

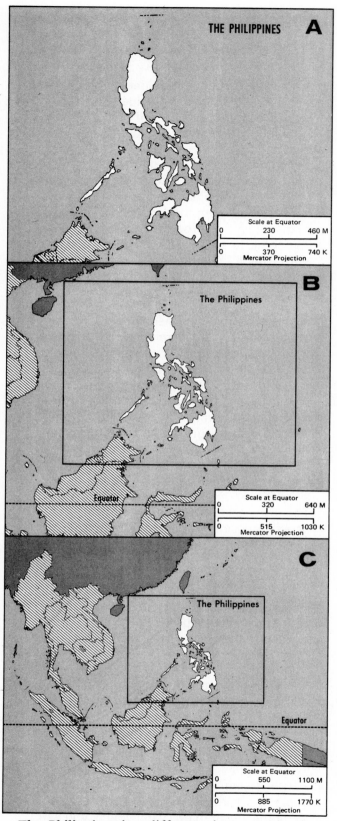

The Philippines is a different size on each of the three maps above. This is because one inch on each of these maps represents a different distance on the surface of the earth.

Learning Map Skills

The earth is a sphere. Our earth is round like a ball. We call any object with this shape a sphere. The earth is, of course, a very large sphere. Its diameter* is about 8,000 miles (12,874 kilometers*). Its circumference is about 25,000 miles (40,233 kilometers). The earth is not quite a perfect sphere, however, for it is slightly flattened at the North and South poles.

Globes and maps. The globe in your classroom is also a sphere. It is a model of the earth. The surface of the globe shows the shapes of the earth's landmasses and bodies of water. It also shows their locations. Globes are made with the North Pole at the top, but they are usually tilted to show the way the earth is tilted. Maps are flat drawings that represent part or all of the earth's surface.

Scale. Globes and maps give information about distance. When you use them, you need to know what distance on the earth is represented by a given distance on the globe or map. This relationship is called the scale. The scale of a globe or map may be expressed in several different ways.

On most maps, the scale is shown by a small drawing. For example:

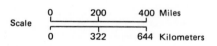

Sometimes, the scale is expressed in this way: 1 inch = 400 miles (644 kilometers).

Scale is often shown in another way, especially on globes and large maps. For example: 1:10,000,000. These numbers mean that any given distance on the globe or map represents a distance on the earth that is ten million times as large. When the scale is shown in this way, you may use any kind of measuring unit you wish. If you choose the inch, then one inch on the globe or map equals ten million inches on the earth, or about 158 miles. If, however, you prefer to use measuring units from the metric* system, then one centimeter* on the globe or map would represent ten million centimeters on the earth, or 100 kilometers.

*See Glossary

Locating places on the earth. Map makers, travelers, and other curious people have always wanted to know just where certain places are located. Over the years, a very accurate way of giving such information has been worked out. This system is used all over the world.

In order to work out a system for locating anything, you need starting points and a measuring unit. The North and South poles and the equator are the starting points for the system we use to locate places on the earth. The measuring unit for our system is called the degree (°).

Parallels show latitude. When we want to locate a place on the earth, we first find out how far it is north or south of the equator. This distance measured in degrees is called north or south latitude. The equator represents zero latitude. The North Pole is located at 90 degrees north latitude, and the South Pole is at 90 degrees south latitude.

All points on the earth that have the same latitude are the same distance from the equator. A line connecting such points is called a parallel. This is because it is parallel to the equator. (See illustration D, below.)

Meridians show longitude. After we know the latitude of a place, we need to know its location in an east-west direction. This is called its longitude. The lines that show longitude are called meridians. They are drawn so as to connect the North and South poles. (See illustration E, below.) Longitude is measured from the meridian that passes through Greenwich, England. This line of zero longitude is called the prime meridian. Distance east or west of this meridian measured in degrees is called east or west longitude. The meridian of 180 degrees west longitude is the same as the one of 180 degrees east longitude. This is because 180 degrees is exactly halfway around the world from the prime meridian.

Locating places on a globe. The location of a certain place might be given to you like this: 30°N 90°W. This means that this place is located 30 degrees north of the equator, and 90 degrees west of the prime meridian. See if you can find this place on the globe in your classroom. It is helpful to remember that parallels and meridians are drawn every ten or fifteen degrees on most globes.

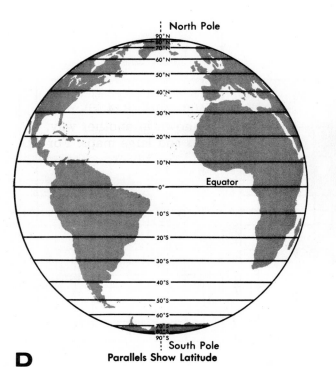

D **Parallels Show Latitude**

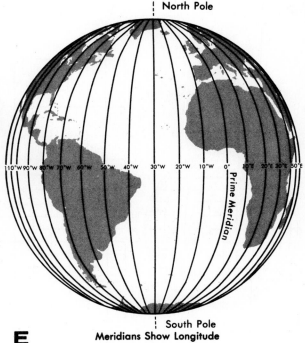

E **Meridians Show Longitude**

The round earth on a flat map. An important fact about a sphere is that you cannot flatten out its surface perfectly. To prove this, you might perform an experiment. Cut an orange in half and scrape away the fruit. You will not be able to press either piece of orange peel flat without crushing it. If you cut one piece in half, however, you can press these smaller pieces nearly flat. Next, cut one of these pieces of peel into three sections, or gores, shaped like those in illustration F, below. You will be able to press these small sections quite flat.

A map like the one shown in illustration F can be made by cutting the surface of a globe into twelve pieces shaped like the smallest sections of your orange peel. Such a map would be fairly accurate. However, an "orange-peel" map is not an easy map to use, because the continents and oceans are split apart.

A flat map can never show the earth's surface as truthfully as a globe can. On globes, shape, size, distance, and direction are all accurate. Although a single flat map of the world cannot be drawn to show all four of these things correctly, flat maps can be made that show some of these things accurately. The various ways of drawing maps of the world to show different things correctly are called map projections.

The Mercator* projection. Illustration G, below, shows a world map called a Mercator projection. When you compare this map

A Round Globe on a Flat Surface

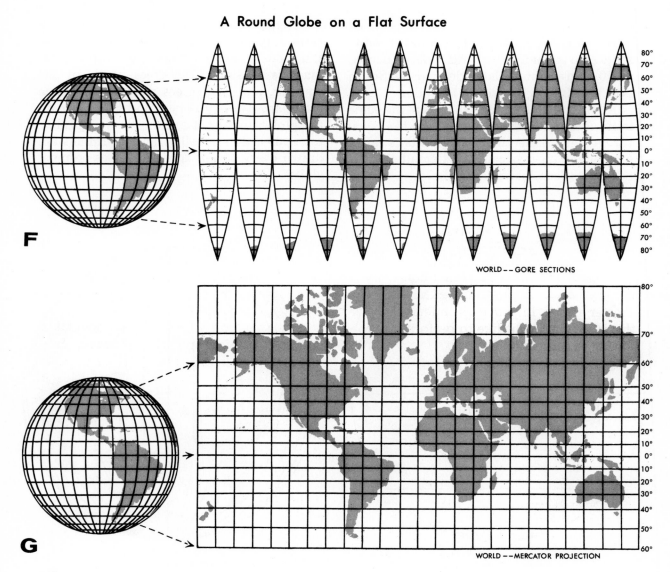

WORLD -- GORE SECTIONS

WORLD -- MERCATOR PROJECTION

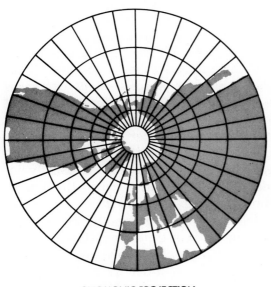

GNOMONIC PROJECTION

H

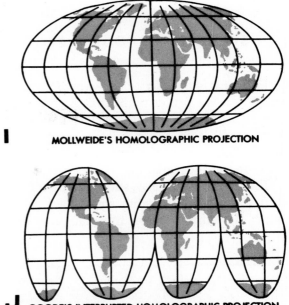

I MOLLWEIDE'S HOMOLOGRAPHIC PROJECTION

J GOODE'S INTERRUPTED HOMOLOGRAPHIC PROJECTION

with a globe, you can see that continents, islands, and oceans have almost the right shape. On this kind of map, however, North America seems larger than Africa, which is not true. On Mercator maps, lands far from the equator appear larger than they are.

Because they show true directions, Mercator maps are especially useful to navigators. For instance, the city of Lisbon, Portugal, lies almost exactly east of Baltimore, Maryland. A Mercator map shows that a ship could reach Lisbon by sailing from Baltimore straight east across the Atlantic Ocean.

The shortest route. Strangely enough, the best way to reach Lisbon from Baltimore is not by traveling straight east. There is a shorter route. In order to understand why this is so, you might like to perform the following experiment.

On your classroom globe, locate Lisbon and Baltimore. Both cities lie just south of the 40th parallel. Take a piece of string and connect the two cities. Let the string follow the true east-west direction of the 40th parallel. Now, draw the string tight. Notice that it passes far to the north of the 40th parallel. The path of the tightened string is the shortest route between Baltimore and Lisbon. The shortest route between any two points on the earth is called the great* circle route.

The gnomonic (nō mon′ik) projection. Using a globe and a piece of string is not a very handy or accurate way of finding great circle routes. Instead, sailors and fliers use a special kind of map called the gnomonic projection. (See illustration H, above.) On this kind of map, the great circle route between any two places can be found simply by drawing a straight line between them.

Equal-area projections. Mercator and gnomonic maps are both very useful, but they do not show true areas. They cannot be used when you want to compare areas in different parts of the world. This is because sections of these maps that are the same size do not always represent the same amounts of the earth's surface.

Maps that do show true areas are called equal-area projections. If one square inch of such a map represents a certain number of square miles on the earth's surface, then every other square inch of the map will represent an equal number of square miles on the earth. In order to draw an equal-area map of the world on a flat surface, the shapes of the landmasses and bodies of water must be distorted. (See illustration I, above.) To avoid this, some equal-area maps are broken, or interrupted. The breaks are arranged to fall at places that are not important. (See illustration J, above.)

SPECIAL-PURPOSE MAPS

Maps that show part of the earth. For some purposes, we prefer maps that do not show the entire surface of the earth. A map of a very small area can be drawn more accurately than a map of a large area. It can also include more details.

Illustration K, below, shows a photograph and a map of the same small part of the earth. The drawings on the map that show the shape and location of things on the earth are called symbols. The small drawing that shows directions is called a compass* rose.

Maps for special purposes. Maps can show the location of many different kinds of things. For instance, a map can show what minerals are found in certain places, or what crops are grown. A small chart that lists the symbols and their meanings is usually included on a map. This is called the legend, or key. (See map M, below.)

Symbols on some geography maps stand for the amounts of things in different places. For instance, map L, below, gives information about the number of people in the southwestern part of the United States. The key tells the meaning of the symbols, which in this case are dots and circles.

On different maps, the same symbol may stand for different things and amounts. For example, each dot on map L stands for 10,000 persons. On other maps, a dot might represent 5,000 sheep or 1,000 bushels of wheat.

There are other ways of giving information about quantity. For example, various designs or patterns may be used on a rainfall map to indicate the areas that receive different amounts of rain each year.

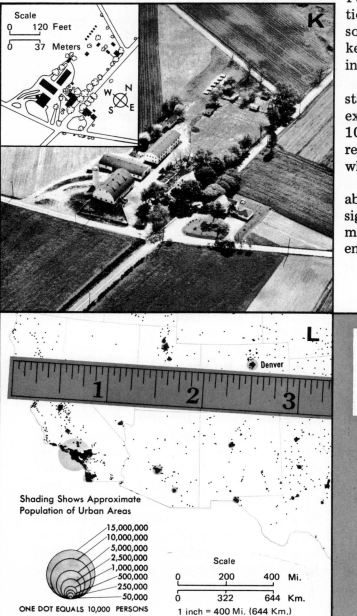

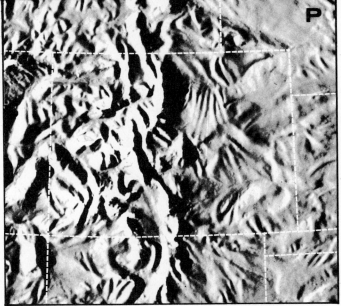

RELIEF MAPS

Some globes and maps show the roughness of the earth's surface. From a jet plane, you can see that the earth's surface is irregular. You can see mountains and valleys, hills and plains. For some purposes, globes and maps that show these things are needed. They are called relief globes and maps.

Since globes are three-dimensional models of the earth, you may wonder why most globes do not show the roughness of the earth's surface. The reason for this is that the highest mountain on the earth is not very large when it is compared with the earth's diameter. Even a very large globe would be almost perfectly smooth.

In order to make a relief globe or map, you must use a different scale for the height of the land. For example, you might start with a large flat map. One inch on your flat map may represent a distance of 100 miles (161 kilometers) on the earth. Now you are going to make a model of a mountain on your map. On the earth, this mountain is two miles (3.2 kilometers) high. If you let one inch represent this height on the earth, your mountain should rise one inch above the flat surface of your map. Other mountains and hills should be modeled on this same scale.

By photographing relief globes and maps, flat maps can be made that show the earth much as it looks from an airplane. Maps N and O, at the top of this page, are photographs of a relief globe. Map P is a photograph of a relief map.

Topographic maps. Another kind of map that shows the roughness of the earth's

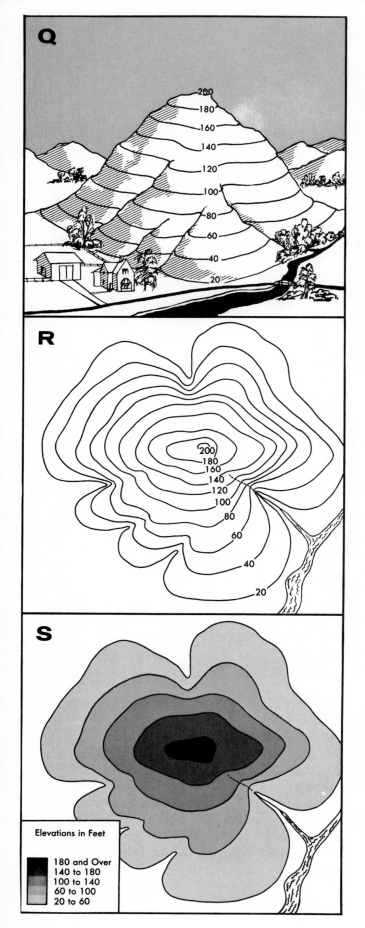

Elevations in Feet

- 180 and Over
- 140 to 180
- 100 to 140
- 60 to 100
- 20 to 60

surface is called a topographic, or contour, map. On this kind of map, lines are drawn to show different heights of the earth's surface. These are called contour lines. Illustrations Q, R, and S help to explain how topographic maps are made. Elevations are given in feet.

Illustration Q is a drawing of a hill. Around the bottom of the hill is our first contour line. This line connects all the points at the base of the hill that are exactly twenty feet above sea level. Higher up the hill, another contour line is drawn, connecting all the points that are exactly forty feet above sea level. A line is also drawn at a height of sixty feet. Other lines are drawn every twenty feet to the top of the hill. Since the hill is shaped somewhat like a cone, each contour line is shorter than the one just below it.

Illustration R shows how the contour lines in the drawing of the hill (Q) can be used to make a topographic map. This map gives us a great deal of information about the hill. Since each line is labeled with the height it represents, you can tell how high the different parts of the hill are. It is important to remember that land does not really rise in layers, as you might think when you look at a topographic map. Wherever the contour lines are far apart, you can be sure that the land slopes gently. Where they are close together, the slope is steep. With practice, you can picture the land in your mind as you look at such a map. Topographic maps are especially useful to people who design such things as roads and buildings.

On a topographic map, the spaces between the contour lines may be filled in with different shades of gray. If a different shade of gray were used for each different height of land shown in map R, there would be ten shades. It would be very hard for you to tell these different shades of gray apart. Therefore on map S, at left, black and four shades of gray were used to show differences in height of forty feet. The key box shows the height of the land represented by the different shades. On some topographic maps, colors are used to represent different heights.

176

Learning Social Studies Skills

What is a skill? A skill is something that you have learned to do well. To learn some skills, such as swimming, you must train the muscles of your arms and legs. To learn others, such as typing, you must train your fingers. Still other skills require you to train your mind. For example, reading with understanding is a skill that requires much mental training. The skills that you use in the social studies are largely mental skills.

Why are skills important? Mastering different skills will help you to have a more satisfying life. You will be healthier and enjoy your leisure time more if you develop skills needed to take part in various sports. By developing artistic skills, you will be able to express your feelings more fully. It is even more important for you to develop skills of the mind. These skills are the tools that you will use in obtaining and using the knowledge you need to live successfully in today's world.

To develop a skill, you must practice it correctly. If you ask fine athletes or musicians how they gained their skills, they will say, "Through practice." To develop skills of the mind, you must practice also. Remember, however, that a person cannot become a good ballplayer if he or she keeps throwing the ball incorrectly. The same thing is true of mental skills. To master them, you must practice them correctly.

The following pages contain suggestions about how to perform correctly several important skills needed in the social studies. Study these skills carefully, and use them.

How To Find Information You Need

Each day of your life you seek information. Sometimes you want to know certain facts just because you are curious. Most of the time, however, you want information for some special purpose. If your hobby is baseball, for example, you may want to know how to figure batting averages. If you collect stamps, you need to know how to identify the countries they come from. As a student in today's world, you need information for many purposes. As an adult, you will need even more knowledge to live successfully in tomorrow's world.

You may wonder how you can possibly learn all the facts you are going to need during your lifetime. The answer is that you can't. Therefore, knowing how to find information when you need it is of vital importance to you. Following are suggestions for locating good sources of information and for using these sources to find the facts that you need.

Written Sources of Information

1. Books. You may be able to find the information you need in books that you have at home or in your classroom. To see if a textbook or other nonfiction book has the information you need, look at the table of contents and the index.

Sometimes, you will need to go to your school or community library to locate books that contain the information you want. To make the best use of a library, you should learn to use the card catalog. This is a file that contains information about the books in the library. Each nonfiction book has at least three cards, filed in alphabetical order. One is for the title, one is for the author, and one is for the subject of the book. Each card gives the book's special number. This number will help you to find the book, since all the nonfiction books in the library are arranged on the shelves in numerical order. If you cannot find a book you want, the librarian will be glad to help you.

2. Reference volumes. You will find much useful information in special books known as reference volumes. These include dictionaries, encyclopedias, atlases, and other special books. Some companies publish a book each year with statistics and general information about the

events of the preceding year. Such books are usually called yearbooks, annuals, or almanacs.

3. <u>Newspapers and magazines.</u> These are important sources of up-to-date information. Sometimes you will want to look for information in papers or magazines that you do not have at home. You can usually find the ones you want at the library.

The *Readers' Guide to Periodical Literature*, which is available in most libraries, will direct you to magazine articles about the subject you are investigating. This is a series of volumes that list articles by title, author, and subject. In the front of each volume is an explanation of the abbreviations used to indicate the different magazines and their dates.

4. <u>Booklets, pamphlets, and bulletins.</u> Many materials of this type are available from local and state governments, as well as from our federal government. Chambers of commerce, travel bureaus, trade organizations, private companies, and embassies of foreign countries publish materials that contain much information.

Many booklets and bulletins give accurate information. You should remember, however, that some of them are intended to promote certain products or ideas. Information obtained from such sources should be checked carefully.

Reading for Information

The following suggestions will help you save time and effort when you are looking for information in books and other written materials.

1. <u>Use the table of contents and the index.</u> The table of contents appears at the beginning of the book and generally is a list of the chapters in the book. By looking at this list, you can usually tell whether the book has the type of information you need.

The index is a more detailed list of the topics that are discussed in the book. It will help you locate the pages on which specific facts are discussed. In most books, the index is at the back. Encyclopedias often include the index in a separate volume, however.

At the beginning of an index, you will usually find an explanation that makes it easier to use. For example, the explanation at the beginning of the Index for *Japan* tells you that *p* means picture and *m* means map.

The topics, or entries, in the index are arranged in alphabetical order. To locate all the information you need, you may have to look under more than one entry. For example, to find out what pages in this book discuss cities, look up the entry for cities. Also, look up the entry for a specific city, such as Tokyo.

2. <u>Skim the written material to see if it contains the information you need.</u> Before you begin reading a chapter or a page, skim it to see if it has the information you need. In this way you will not run the risk of wasting time reading something that is of little or no value to you. When you skim, you look mainly for topic headings, topic sentences, and key words. For example, imagine you are looking for the answer to the question: "How did the Meiji leaders help Japan to become a modern country?" First, you might look in the history section for a topic heading that mentions Japan becoming a modern country. After finding this topic heading, you might look for a key term such as "Meiji leaders."

3. <u>Read carefully when you think you have located the information you need.</u> When you think you have found the page that contains the information you are looking for, read it carefully. Does it really tell you what you want to know? If not, you will need to look further.

Other Ways of Obtaining Information

1. <u>Direct experience.</u> What you observe or experience for yourself may be a good source of information if you have observed carefully and remembered accurately. Firsthand information can often be obtained by visiting places

in your community or nearby, such as museums, factories, or government offices.

2. Radio and television. Use the listings in your local newspaper to find programs about the subjects in which you are interested.

3. Movies, filmstrips, recordings, and slides. Materials on a great variety of subjects are available. They can be obtained from schools, libraries, museums, and private companies.

4. Resource people. Sometimes, you will be able to obtain information by interviewing a person who has special knowledge. On occasion, you may wish to invite someone to speak to your class and answer questions.

Evaluating Information

During your lifetime, you will constantly need to evaluate what you see, hear, and read. Information is not true or significant simply because it is presented on television or is written in a book, magazine, or newspaper. The following suggestions will help you in evaluating information.

Learn to tell the difference between primary and secondary sources of information. A primary source of information is a firsthand record. For example, a photograph taken of an event while it is happening is a primary source. So is the report you write about a field trip you take. Original documents, such as the Constitution of the United States, are primary sources, also.

A secondary source is a secondhand report. For example, if you write a report about what someone else told you he or she saw, your report will be a secondary source of information. Another example of a secondary source is a history book.

Advanced scholars like to use primary sources whenever possible. However, these sources are often difficult to obtain. Most students in elementary and high school use secondary sources. You should always be aware that you are using secondhand information when you use a secondary source.

Find out who said it and when it was said. The next step in evaluating information is to ask, "Who said it?" Was she a scholar with special training in the subject about which she wrote? Was he a newsman with a reputation for careful reporting of the facts?

Another question you should ask is, "When was it said?" Changes take place rapidly in our world, and the information you are using may be out of date. For example, suppose you are looking for information about a country. If you use an encyclopedia that is five years old, much of the information you find will be inaccurate.

Find out if it is mainly fact or opinion. The next step in evaluating information is to decide whether it is based on facts or whether it mainly consists of unsupported opinions. You can do this best if you are aware of these three types of statements.

1. Statements of fact that can be checked. For example, "Voters in the United States choose their representatives by secret ballot" is a statement of fact that can be checked by observing how voting is carried on in different parts of our country.

2. Inferences, or conclusions that are based on facts. The statement "The people of the United States live in a democracy" is an inference. This inference is based on the fact that the citizens choose their representatives by secret ballot, and on other facts that can be proved. It is important to remember that inferences can be false or only partly true.

3. Value judgments, or opinions. The statement "It is always wrong for a country to go to war" is a value judgment. Since a value judgment is an opinion, you need to examine it

Seven Propaganda Tricks

People who use propaganda have learned many ways of presenting information to influence you in the direction they wish. Seven propaganda tricks to watch for are listed below.

Name Calling. Giving a label that is disliked or feared, such as "un-American," to an organization, a person, or an idea. This trick often persuades people to reject something they know nothing about.

Glittering Generalities. Trying to win support by using fine-sounding phrases, such as "the best deal in town" or "the American way." These phrases have no clear meaning when you stop and think about them.

Transfer. Connecting a person, product, or idea with something that people already feel strongly about. For example, displaying a picture of a church next to a speaker to give the impression that he or she is honest and trustworthy.

Testimonial. Getting well-known persons or organizations to announce in public their support of a person, product, or idea.

Plain Folks. Trying to win support by appearing to be an ordinary person who can be trusted. For example, a political candidate may try to win people's confidence by giving the impression that he or she is a good parent who loves children and dogs.

Card Stacking. Giving the wrong impression by giving only part of the facts about a person, product, or idea. For example, giving favorable facts, and leaving out unfavorable ones.

Bandwagon. Trying to win support by saying that "everybody knows that" or "everyone is doing this."

---

very critically. On what facts and inferences is it based? For example, what facts and conclusions do you think form the basis of the opinion: "It is always wrong for a country to go to war"? Do you agree or disagree with these conclusions? Reliable writers or reporters are careful to let their readers know which statements are their own opinions. They also try to base their opinions as much as possible on facts that can be proved.

Find out why it was said. The next step in evaluating information is to find out the purpose for which it was prepared. Many books and articles are prepared in an honest effort to give you accurate information. For example, scientists writing about a new scientific discovery will usually try to report their findings as accurately as possible, and they will be careful to distinguish between what they have actually observed and the conclusions they have drawn from these facts.

Some information, however, is prepared mainly to persuade people to believe or act a certain way. Information of this kind is called propaganda.

Some propaganda is used to promote causes that are generally considered good. A picture that shows Smokey the Bear and the words "Only *you* can prevent forest fires" is an example of this kind of propaganda.

Propaganda is also used to make people support causes they would not agree with if they knew more about them. This kind of propaganda may consist of information that is true, partly true, or false. Even when it is true, however, the information may be presented in such a way as to mislead you.

Propaganda generally appeals to people's emotions rather than to their reasoning ability. For this reason, you should learn to identify information that is propaganda. Then you can think about it calmly and clearly, and evaluate it intelligently.

Making Reports

There are many occasions when you need to share information or ideas with others. Sometimes you will need to do this in writing. Other times you will need to do it orally. One of the best ways to develop your writing and speaking skills is by making oral and written reports. The success of your report will depend on how well you have organized your material. It will also depend on your skill in presenting it. Here are some guidelines that will help you in preparing a good report.

Decide upon a goal. Have your purpose clearly in mind. Are you mainly interested in communicating information? Do you want to give your own viewpoint on a subject, or are you trying to persuade other people to agree with you?

Find the information you need. Be sure to use more than one source. If you are not sure how to locate information about your topic, read the suggestions on pages 177-179 of this Skills Manual.

Take good notes. To remember what you have read, you must take notes. Before you begin taking notes, however, you will need to make a list of the questions you want your report to answer. As you do research, write down the facts that answer these questions. You may find some interesting and important facts that do not answer any of your questions. If you feel that they might be useful in your report, write them down, too. Your notes should be brief and in your own words except when you want to use exact quotations. When you use a quotation, be sure to put quotation marks around it.

You will be able to make the best use of your notes if you write them on file cards. Use a separate card for each statement or group of statements that answers one of your questions. To remember where your information came from, write on each card the title, author, and date of the source. When you have finished taking notes, group the cards according to the questions they answer. This will help you arrange your material in logical order.

Make an outline. After you have reviewed your notes, make an outline. This is a general plan that shows the order and the relationship of the ideas you want to include in your report. The first step in making an outline is to pick out the main ideas. These will be the main headings in your outline. (See sample outline below.) Next, list under each of these headings the ideas and facts that support or explain it. These related ideas are called subheadings. As you arrange your information, ask yourself the following questions.

a. Is there one main idea that I must put first because everything else depends on it?

b. Have I arranged my facts in such a way as to show relationships among them?

c. Are there some ideas that will be clearer if they are discussed after other ideas have been explained?

d. Have I included enough facts so that I can complete my outline with a summary statement or a logical conclusion?

When you have completed your first outline, you may find that some parts of it are skimpy. If so, you may wish to do more research. When you are satisfied that you have enough information, make your final outline. Remember that this outline will serve as the basis of your finished report.

Example of an outline. The author of this feature prepared the following outline before writing "Making Reports."

I. Introduction
II. Deciding upon a goal
III. Finding information
IV. Taking notes
    A. List main ideas to be researched
    B. Write on file cards facts that support or explain these ideas
    C. Group cards according to main ideas
V. Making an outline
    A. Purpose of an outline
    B. Guidelines for arranging information
    C. Sample outline of this section
VI. Preparing a written report
VII. Presenting an oral report

Special guidelines for a written report. As a guide in writing your report, use the outline you have prepared. The following suggestions will help you to make your report interesting and clear.

Create word pictures that your readers can see in their minds. Before you begin to write, imagine that you are going to make a movie of the subject you plan to write about. What scenes would you like to show on the screen? Next, think of the words that will create these same pictures in your readers' minds.

Group your sentences into good paragraphs. It is usually best to begin a paragraph with a topic sentence that says to the reader, "This is what you will learn about in this paragraph." The other sentences in the paragraph should help to support or explain the topic sentence.

A sample paragraph. Below is a sample paragraph from this book. The topic sentence has been underlined. Notice how clear it is and how well the other sentences support it. Also notice how many pictures the paragraph puts in your mind.

Hills and mountains cover most of the land in Japan. This rugged, island country is the upper part of a great mountain range that rose from the bottom of the ocean. Millions of years ago, movements deep within the earth cracked the layers of rock at the bottom of the ocean and pushed them upward. This process took place over a long period of time. The high peaks and ridges that were finally thrust above the surface of the water formed the islands of Japan.

Other guidelines. There are two other things to remember in writing a good report. First, use the dictionary to find the spelling of words you are doubtful about. Second, make a list of the sources of information you used, and include it at the beginning or end of your report. This list is called a bibliography.

Special guidelines for an oral report. When you are going to give a report orally, you will also want to organize your information in a logical order by making an outline. Prepare notes to guide you during your talk. These notes should be complete enough to help you remember all the points you want to make. You may even write out portions of your report that you prefer to read.

When you present your report, speak directly to your audience. Pronounce your words correctly and distinctly. Remember to speak slowly enough for your listeners to follow what you are saying, and use a tone of voice that will hold their interest. Stand up straight, but try not to be too stiff. The only way to improve your speaking skills is to practice them correctly.

Holding a Group Discussion

One of the important ways in which you learn is by exchanging ideas with other people. You do this frequently in informal conversation. You are likely to learn more, however, when you take part in the special kind of group conversation that we call a discussion. A discussion is more orderly than a conversation, and it usually has a definite, serious purpose. This purpose may be the sharing of information or the solving of a problem. In order to reach its goal, the discussion group must arrive at a conclusion or make a decision of some kind.

A discussion is more likely to be successful when those who take part in it observe the following guidelines.

1. Be prepared. Think about the topic to be discussed ahead of time. Prepare for the discussion by reading and taking notes. You may also want to make an outline of the ideas you want to share with the group.

2. Take part. Contribute to the discussion; express your ideas clearly and concisely. Be sure that the statements you make and the questions you ask deal with the topic being discussed.

3. Listen and think. Listen thoughtfully to others. Encourage all of the members of the discussion group to express their ideas. Do not make up your mind about a question or a problem until all of the facts have been given.

4. Be courteous. When you speak, address the entire group. Ask and answer questions politely. When you disagree with someone, point out your reasons calmly and in a friendly way.

Working With Others

In school and throughout life, you will find that there are many projects that can be done better by a group than by one person working alone. Some of these projects would take too long to finish if they were done by a single individual. Others have different parts that can be done best by people with different talents.

Before your group begins a project, you should decide several matters. First, determine exactly what you are trying to accomplish. Second, decide what part of the project each person should do. Third, schedule when the project is to be completed.

The group will do a better job and reach its goals more quickly if each person follows these suggestions.

1. Do your part. Remember that the success of your project depends on every member of the group. Be willing to do your share of the work and to accept your share of the responsibility.

2. Follow the rules. Help the group decide on sensible rules, and then follow them. When a difference of opinion cannot be settled by discussion, make a decision by majority vote.

3. Share your ideas. Be willing to share your ideas and talents with the group. When you submit an idea for discussion, be prepared to see it criticized or even rejected. At the same time, have the courage to stick up for a principle or a belief that is really important to you.

4. Respect others. Remember that every person is an individual with different beliefs and talents. Give the other members of the group a chance to be heard, and be ready to appreciate their work and ideas.

5. Be friendly, thoughtful, helpful, and cheerful. Try to express your opinions seriously and sincerely without hurting others or losing their respect. Listen politely to the ideas of others.

6. Learn from your mistakes. Look for ways in which you can be a better group member the next time you work with others on a project.

Building Your Vocabulary

When you do research in many different types of reading materials, you are likely to find several words you have never seen before. If you skip over these words, the chances are that you will not fully understand what you are reading. The following suggestions will help you to discover the meanings of new words and build your vocabulary.

1. See how the word is used in the sentence. When you come to a new word, don't stop reading. Read on beyond the new word to see if you can discover any clues to what its meaning might be. Trying to figure out the meaning of a word from the way it is used may not give you the exact definition. However, it will give you a general idea of what the word means.

2. Sound out the word. Break the word up into syllables, and try to pronounce it. When you say the word aloud, you may find that you know it after all but have simply never seen it in print.

3. Look in the dictionary. When you think you have figured out what a word means and how it is pronounced, check with the dictionary. Have you pronounced it correctly? Did you decide upon the right definition? Remember, most words have several meanings. Do you know which meaning should be used?

4. Make a list of the new words you learn. In your own words, write a definition of each word you include in your list. Review this list from time to time.

GLOSSARY

Complete Pronunciation Key

The pronunciation of each word is shown just after the word in this way: **barnacles** (bär′nə kəls). The letters and signs used are pronounced as in the words below. The mark ′ is placed after a syllable with a primary or strong accent, as in the example above. The mark ′ after a syllable shows a secondary or lighter accent, as in **Tokugawa**((tō ′kù gä′wä).

a	hat, cap	j	jam, enjoy	u	cup, butter
ā	age, face	k	kind, seek	ù	full, put
ã	care, air	l	land, coal	ü	rule, move
ä	father, far	m	me, am	ū	use, music
		n	no, in		
b	bad, rob	ng	long, bring		
ch	child, much			v	very, save
d	did, red	o	hot, rock	w	will, woman
		ō	open, go	y	young, yet
		ô	order, all	z	zero, breeze
e	let, best	oi	oil, voice	zh	measure, seizure
ē	equal, see	ou	house, out		
ėr	term, learn				
		p	paper, cup		
f	fat, if	r	run, try	ə	represents:
g	go, bag	s	say, yes	a	in about
h	he, how	sh	she, rush	e	in taken
		t	tell, it	i	in pencil
i	it, pin	th	thin, both	o	in lemon
ī	ice, five	ŦH	then, smooth	u	in circus

acre. A unit of area. A football field covers about one and one-third acres.

Allied. Refers to Allies, the group of countries that defeated the Axis nations in World War II. See **World War II.**

bamboo. Any one of several woody or tree-like plants of the grass family.

barnacles (bär′nə kəls). Shellfish that live in the ocean. They sometimes attach themselves to hulls of ships.

battledore and shuttlecock. A game similar to badminton. The players bat a feathered cork, called a shuttlecock, back and forth between them. They use small rackets, called battledores.

bauxite (bôk′sīt). An ore that is the chief source of aluminum. Bauxite may occur as a rocklike or claylike material.

British Commonwealth (now called Commonwealth of Nations). A voluntary association of independent nations and their dependencies, joined together for mutual benefit. The Commonwealth is headed by the British crown.

Buddha (bùd′ ə), **Siddhartha Gautama** (siddär′tə gou′tə mə), 563?-?483 B.C. The founder of the Buddhist religion. He taught that selfish desires are the cause of all sorrow, and that by getting rid of these desires a person can gain perfect peace and happiness.

Buddhism (bùd′iz əm). A religion founded by Siddhartha Gautama Buddha. See **Buddha.**

Buddhist (bùd′ist). Refers to the religion founded by Buddha, and to its followers. See **Buddha.**

bullock. An ox often used as a work animal.

centimeter (sen′ tə mē′ tər). A unit in the metric system for measuring length. It is equal to about .39 inch. See **metric system.**

circumference (sėr kum′fər əns). The distance around an object or a geometric figure, especially a circle or a sphere.

clan. A group of people who claim to be descended from the same ancestor. Clan members have a strong feeling of belonging together.

coke. A fuel made by roasting coal in special airtight ovens. Coke, which burns at a very high temperature, is needed for the production of iron from iron ore.

coking coal. Coal that is suitable for being made into coke. See **coke.**

Cold War. The general term "cold war" refers to any conflict between different nations or groups of people that does not involve violence. Such a conflict is called "cold" because it is fought largely with propaganda and with economic and social pressures rather than with guns and bombs. When capitalized, the term "Cold War" refers to the conflict between Communist and non-Communist countries that began after World War II. During the Cold War, actual fighting took place in certain countries, mainly Korea and Vietnam.

Colombo (kə lum′ bō) **Plan.** A program to aid the economic development of countries in South and Southeast Asia. Provides advice and money, trains workers, and carries on research in agriculture and industry.

compass rose. A small drawing included on a map to show directions. A compass rose is often used as a decoration. Here are three examples of compass roses:

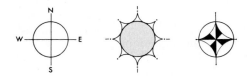

cooperative. See **farmers' cooperative.**

copper. A reddish brown metal that can easily be worked into different shapes. It is one of the best conductors of electricity.

diameter (dī am′ə tər). A straight line that goes through the center of a geometric figure, especially a circle or sphere. The line joins two opposite points on the figure.

dictatorship. A government in which all ruling power is held by a single leader or by a small group of leaders.

diesel (dē′zəl) **engines.** Engines that burn fuel oils. Named after the German inventor Rudolf Diesel.

diesel (dē′zəl) **locomotive.** A locomotive powered by electricity that is produced by a generator run by a diesel engine. See **diesel engines.**

Diet (dī′ət). The national lawmaking assembly of Japan.

ecology (ē kol′ ə jē). Refers to all the various relationships between living things (plants, animals, and human beings) and between living things and their environment. Also, the scientific study of these relationships.

equator (i kwā′ tər). An imaginary line around the earth, dividing it into a northern half and a southern half.

farmers' cooperative. A business organization owned by a group of farmers who share the profits it makes. In Japan, cooperatives buy products from farmers and sell them goods they need. Other services offered by farm cooperatives in Japan are credit, joint use of warehouses, and joint use of farm equipment.

Formosa (fôr mō′ sə). Also called Taiwan (tī′ wän′). An island off the southeastern coast of the Chinese mainland.

generator. A machine that changes mechanical energy into electrical energy.

glacier (glā′ shər). A great mass of slowly moving ice that has been formed in a region where more snow falls in winter than melts in summer.

great circle. Any imaginary circle around the earth that divides its surface exactly in half. The equator, for example, is a great circle. The shortest route between any two points on the earth always lies on a great circle.

hectare (hek′tār). A unit in the metric system for measuring area. It is equal to about 2.47 acres. See **metric system.**

illiterate. Unable to read or write.

Indochina. The part of Southeast Asia in which Laos, Democratic Kampuchea (Cambodia), and Vietnam are now located. (See map, pages 6 and 7.)

Kabuki (kä bü′kē). A popular form of traditional Japanese drama that combines the arts of dancing, music, and acting.

Kamakura (käm′ ə kür′ ə). A city on the eastern coast of Honshu, south of Tokyo. From 1192 until 1333, Kamakura was the capital of the shogunate.

kilometer (kə lom′ə tər). A unit in the metric system for measuring length. It is equal to .62 mile. See **metric system.**

kimono (kə mō′ nə). A loose robe with wide sleeves and a broad sash. It is worn by both men and women in Japan.

Korea. A peninsula in eastern Asia. Korea is occupied by North Korea and South Korea, which were formerly united. Korea was annexed by Japan in 1910. Before the end of World War II, the Allies declared their intention of restoring Korean independence. The United States and the Soviet Union agreed to divide the country temporarily at the 38th parallel, with the Soviets accepting surrender of Japanese troops in the north and the Americans doing the same in the south. After the war, the Soviet Union and the United States could not reach agreement on plans for reuniting the country. Korea remains divided, with a Communist government in the north and a non-Communist government in the south.

Korean War. The conflict, lasting from 1950 until 1953, between Communist and anti-Communist forces in Korea. See **Korea.** In 1950, Communist troops from North Korea unexpectedly invaded South Korea. United Nations forces, consisting largely of Americans and South Koreans, but including troops from many other countries, forced the North Koreans back. The cease-fire agreement that brought the Korean War to a close set the boundary between North and South Korea approximately along the 38th parallel.

lacquer (lak′ər). Any one of several types of varnish. In Japan and China, a special type of lacquer is made from the sap of the lacquer tree.

lathe. A machine tool that holds such materials as wood or metal while shaping them. The lathe spins the material around at a high rate of speed. A special tool is used to cut, grind, drill, or polish the material as it spins.

lava. Molten, or melted, rock that flows from a volcano. Also, the rock formed by this molten rock when it cools and hardens.

lead. A soft, heavy metal. It is used to make pipes, storage batteries, and many other products.

limestone. A common rock, usually formed from the shells and skeletons of sea animals. Limestone is used for making cement and in the production of iron and steel. (See pages 148-149.) It is also used as a building stone.

literate. Able to read and write.

Manchuria (man chür′ē ə). A large region in northeastern China that is rich in fertile land, timber and mineral resources, and has important heavy industries. Japan, Russia (after 1922, the Soviet Union), and China have been rivals for control of this valuable area in the past.

Meiji (mā′jē). The name given to the reign of Emperor Meiji of Japan, who came to power in 1867 at the age of 15. He died in 1912. During the Meiji era, Japan was transformed from an isolated, agricultural country into an important industrial and military power.

Mercator (mèr kā′ tər) **projection.** One of many possible arrangements of meridians and parallels on which a map of the world may be drawn. Devised by Gerhardus Mercator, a Flemish geographer who lived from 1512 to 1594. On a Mercator map, all meridians are drawn straight up and down, with north at the top. The parallels are drawn straight across, but increasingly farther apart toward the poles.

metric system. A system of measurement used in most countries and by scientists throughout the world. In this system, meter is the basic unit of length. It is equal to 39.37 inches. In the metric system, 100 centimeters equal one meter, and 1000 meters equal one kilometer.

migration. The movement of people out of one region or country and into another, with the intention of making it their permanent home.

miso (mē′sō). A paste made of cooked soybeans, steamed rice, and salt that have been ground together. It is used in making soups and other types of food.

mollusk. A shellfish such as an oyster or a clam.

monsoons. Winds that reverse their direction from season to season.

Nara (när′ə). A city 26 miles east of Osaka. An ancient capital (710-784 A.D.) of Japan. Many Shinto shrines and Buddhist temples are located here.

Occupation. The period of time following World War II when Allied troops,

---

Pronunciation Key: hat, āge, cãre, fär; let, ēqual, tèrm; it, īce; hot, ōpen, ôrder; oil, out; cup, pùt, rüle, ūse; child; long; thin; ᴛʜen; zh, measure; ə represents a in about, e in taken, i in pencil, o in lemon, u in circus. For the complete key, see page 184.

mainly Americans, occupied Japan. The official Occupation lasted from September 2, 1945, to April 28, 1952.

octopuses. Sea animals with soft, bag-shaped bodies and eight long, flexible arms, called tentacles. The octopus is used for food in Japan and other parts of the world.

Okhotsk (ō kotsk′) **Current.** A cold ocean current that flows southward along the eastern coasts of Hokkaido and northern Honshu. (See map, page 35.) This current is also called the Oyashio.

oxygen (ok′sə jən). A colorless, odorless, tasteless gas that makes up about one fifth of the air in the earth's atmosphere. In combination with other substances, oxygen is found in all plants and animals, in water, and in many kinds of rock.

petrochemicals. Chemicals obtained from petroleum or natural gas. Petrochemicals are used in making plastics, fertilizers, and other products.

petroleum. A thick, oily liquid obtained from the earth. It is usually dark brown or greenish black in color. Gasoline, kerosene, and many other products are made from petroleum.

plateau (pla tō′). A large, generally level area of high land.

plywood. Boards made of thin layers of wood that have been glued together. Plywood is used mainly in making furniture and as a building material.

prefecture (prē′fek chər). A political division of Japan similar to a state in the United States. Each of Japan's 47 prefectures has its own local government.

proteins. A group of substances found in all living cells of plants and animals. Living things must have proteins in order to repair damaged cells and build new ones. Good food sources of proteins are eggs, meat, fish, and soybeans.

rayon. Thread or cloth made from cellulose that has been treated with chemicals. The main substance of the cell walls of plants is made up of cellulose. It forms the woody part of plants.

recession. In industrialized countries, a temporary period when there is less business activity than usual and many people are unemployed.

reforestation. The renewing of damaged forests by planting new trees.

reservoir (rez′ər vwär). A lake that stores large quantities of water until needed. A reservoir may be natural or artificial.

Roman alphabet. The alphabet used in writing languages such as English, French, German, and Spanish. Most books, newspapers, and magazines today are written with the Roman alphabet.

samisen (sam′ ə sen). A Japanese musical instrument. A samisen has three strings and is shaped somewhat like a banjo.

scrap. Refers to any pieces of iron or steel that have been discarded, such as worn-out machinery and pieces of steel left over from manufacturing processes.

shogun (shō′gun). The title of the military leaders who ruled Japan during the period between 1192 and 1867.

shrine. A place or object considered sacred.

spatula (spach′ù lə). A tool that has a wide, dull blade. Used to spread paint, putty, cake icing, and other soft substances.

square inch. A unit for measuring area, equal to the area of a square that measures one inch on each side.

square mile. A unit for measuring area, equal to the area of a square that measures one mile on each side. One square mile contains 640 acres. See **acre.**

Sri Lanka (srē′läng′kə). Formerly called Ceylon. An island country in the Indian Ocean close to the southern tip of India. (See map, pages 6 and 7.) It is an independent country.

standard of living. The average level of conditions in a community or country, or the level of conditions that people consider necessary for a happy, satisfying life. In countries with a high standard of living, many different goods and services are considered to be necessities. In countries with a low standard of living, many of these same items are luxuries enjoyed by only a few people.

sulfur (sul′fər). A yellowish chemical element. Used in making rubber, disinfectants, paper pulp, matches, and sulfuric acid and other chemicals.

sulfuric (sul fūr′ik) **acid.** An oily, colorless strong acid. It is an important chemical used in the manufacture of such products as drugs, dyes, and fertilizers.

summary (sum′ər ē) **courts.** Courts of law in which persons accused of minor offenses are tried. The trial is heard by a justice of the peace. In a summary court, legal formalities are omitted in order to settle minor disputes quickly.

synthetic (sin thet′ ik). Refers to certain artificial substances, such as plastics and nylon, developed to replace similar natural materials.

tenant farmers. Farmers who work land owned by someone else and pay rent to the owner, either with money or with a part of what they produce.

three-dimensional (də men′ shən l). Having length, width, and depth. Also, appearing to have depth as well as length and width.

tofu (tō ′füi). A soft cheese made from the milk of soybeans.

tofu-maker. A person who makes tofu.

Tokugawa (tō ′küi gä′wä). Family that controlled Japan from 1603 to 1867. The Tokugawas established a dictatorship in Japan and closed the country off from the rest of the world for more than two centuries.

underdeveloped. Refers to those countries in which most work is done by the muscle power of people and animals. In underdeveloped countries, many natural resources are poorly used and the standard of living is low. In contrast are the developed countries, in which most work is done by power-driven machinery, resources are used extensively, and the general standard of living is high.

United Nations. An organization formed in 1945 to work for world peace. About 150 nations are members. Agencies related to the United Nations work to solve problems in fields such as health, agriculture, and labor.

volcano (vol kā′nō). A crack in the earth's crust through which melted rock and other materials are forced to the surface. The materials forced to the surface form a hill or mountain, which is also called a volcano.

volcano crater. The bowl-shaped opening at the top of a volcano.

war crime. A violation, or breaking, of the laws of war, which generally are accepted by the civilized nations of the world. These laws deal with the treatment of prisoners of war, the duties and rights of neutral nations in time of war, and many other matters.

Western. In this book, refers to Europe and to the United States and other countries whose civilization developed from that of Europe.

Westerners. Refers to people from the Western nations. See **Western.**

wood-block print. A picture or design printed with a block of wood on which a design or picture has been carved. The carved wood block is covered with ink and then paper is pressed against it to print the picture.

World War I, 1914-1918. The first war in history that involved nearly every part of the world. The Central Powers — Germany, Austria, Turkey, and Bulgaria — were defeated by the Allies. These included Great Britain, France, Russia, Japan, and the United States.

World War II, 1939-1945. The second war in history that involved nearly every part of the world. The Allies, which included China, the United States, the United Kingdom, the Soviet Union, and many other countries, defeated the Axis. The Axis included mainly Germany, Italy, and Japan.

zinc. A silvery, bluish white metal. Zinc resists rust and is used chiefly as a protective coating over other metals, especially iron and steel.

Maps and Special Features

INDEX

Explanation of abbreviations used in this Index:

p — picture　　　*m* — map

PRONUNCIATION KEY: hat, āge, cãre, fär; let, ēqual, tėrm; it, īce; hot, ōpen, ôrder; oil, out; cup, pùt, rüle, ūse; child; long; thin; ᴛнen; zh, measure; ə represents a in about, e in taken, i in pencil, o in lemon, u in circus. For the complete key, see page 184.

Acknowledgments

Grateful acknowledgment is made to the following for permission to use the illustrations found in this book:

Black Star: Pages 54-55, 114, and 153

Consulate General of Japan: Pages 28, 36, 68-69, 86, 89, 94-95, 100, 136-137, 149, 150-151, 152, 154-155, and 166

East-West Photographic Agency: Pages 60-61; pages 18-19, 131, and 140-141 by Horace Bristol, Jr.

Foreign Affairs Association of Japan: Pages 42-43 and 143

Freelance Photographers Guild: Pages 56-57

Galloway: Pages 4-5

Harrison Forman: Pages 10-11 and 14-15

Historical Pictures Service: Pages 46-47

International Society for Educational Information, Tokyo, Inc.: Pages 24-25, 44, 49, 52-53, 58-59, 62, 63, 64, 66-67, 72, 78-79, 83, 92-93, 102-103, 104-105, 108-109, 109, 118-119, 122-123, 126-127, 129, 133, 134-135, 139, 150, 160-161, and 162

Japan Air Lines: Page 157

Japan Information Service: Page 147

Japan National Tourist Organization: Pages 32, 40-41, 73, 74-75, 116-117, and 128-129

Japan Trade Center: Pages 144-145

Kyodo Photo Service: Pages 112-113

Orion Press: Pages 2-3, 26-27, 38-39, 50-51, and 60; pages 30-31 by Kazumi Edagawa; pages 34-35 by Juerg Andermatt; page 85 by Hiroshi Ikeda; pages 106-107 by Keikichi Tachibana; page 142 by Yoshiaki Matsuda

Östman, Carl E.: Pages 20-21, 70-71, 77, 80-81, 116, 148, 156, 158, 161, and 164 by H. Fristedt; pages 110-111 by Rolf Clipper

Photo Researchers, Inc.: Page 16 by V. Englebert

Pictorial Parade: Page 56

Publix Pictorial Press: Page 103 by Bob and Ira Spring

Shinano Mainichi Shimbun: Page 132

Shostal Associates, Inc.: Pages 12-13; page 8 by D. J. Forbert

Snow Brand Milk Products Co., Ltd.: Pages 28-29

United Press International Photo: Page 125

Ushijima—Kumamoto, Japan: Pages 90-91 and 91

Zentrale Farbbild Agentur: Page 88; pages 22-23 by S. Sammer; page 96 by Dr. G. Haasch; pages 98-99 by D. Schmidt; page 163 by E. Winter

Grateful acknowledgment is made to Scott, Foresman and Company for the pronunciation system used in this book, which is taken from the Thorndike-Barnhart Dictionary Series.

Grateful acknowledgment is made to the following for permission to use cartographic data in this book: Creative Arts: Top maps on page 175, in the Skills Manual; Nystrom Raised Relief Map Company, Chicago 60618: Page 9, and bottom map on page 175, in the Skills Manual; Panoramic Studios: Pages 6 and 17; Rand McNally & Company: Pages 6-7; United States Department of Commerce, Bureau of the Census: Lower left-hand map on page 174, in the Skills Manual.